California Desert
Byways

Saline Valley Road *(Tour 10)*

California Desert
Byways

Backcountry Drives
For The
Whole Family

By TONY HUEGEL

WILDERNESS PRESS
BERKELEY, CA

First Edition 1995
Second Edition March 2002

Copyright © 2002 by Tony Huegel
All photographs, including cover photographs, by the author
Editor: Tom Winnett
Managing Editor: Jannie Dresser
Cover design and book production: Larry B. Van Dyke
Maps: Jerry Painter

Library of Congress Card Catalog Number *(applied for—not received by publication date)*
ISBN 0-89997-304-3
UPC 7-19609-97304-1

Manufactured in the United States of America

Published by **Wilderness Press**
1200 5th Street
Berkeley, CA 94710-1306
(800) 443-7227; FAX (510) 558-1696
mail@wildernesspress.com

Contact us for a free catalog
Visit our website at **www.wildernesspress.com**

Front cover photo: Red Rock Canyon (Tour 1)
Back cover photo: Cerro Gordo ghost town (Tour 9)
Frontispiece photo: Saline Valley Road (Tour 10)

 Printed on recycled paper

Library of Congress Cataloging-In-Publication Data
(applied for—not received by publication date)

Huegel, Tony.
   California Desert Byways: backcountry drives for the whole family / by
Tony Huegel.—2nd ed.
      p. cm.
   Includes index.
   ISBN 0-89997-304-3
   1.Automobile travel—California deserts and mountain desert
regions—Guidebooks. 2. Sport utility vehicles. 3. California deserts and
mountain desert regions.—Guidebooks. 4. Desert roads—Owens Valley to
the Mexican border, including Mojave and Death Valley deserts. I. Title.
GV 1024 .H   2002
917.94

Disclaimer

California Desert Byways has been prepared to help you enjoy backcountry driving. It assumes you will be driving a high-clearance 4-wheel-drive vehicle that is properly equipped for backcountry travel on unpaved, sometimes unmaintained and primitive backcountry roads. It is not intended to be an exhaustive, all-encompassing authority on backcountry driving, nor is it intended to be your only source of information about the subject. There are risks and dangers that are inevitable when driving in the backcountry. The condition of backcountry roads can deteriorate quickly and substantially at any time. Thus, you may encounter road conditions considerably worse than what is described here. If you drive the roads listed in this book, or any other backcountry roads, you assume all risks, dangers and liability that may result from your actions. The author and the publisher of this book disclaim any and all liability for any injury, loss or damage that you, your passengers or your vehicle may incur.

Exercise the caution and good judgment that visiting the backcountry demands. Bring the proper supplies. Be prepared to deal with accidents, injuries, breakdowns and other problems yourself, because help will almost always be far away and a long time coming.

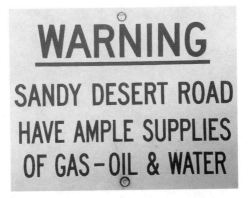

Acknowledgments

No project of this sort is the product of one person's effort alone. Some people helped by suggesting drives. Others helped by reading the material and suggesting improvements and corrections. Still others simply made the whole thing possible.

No one's support and cooperation was more important than that of my wife, Lynn MacAusland, and our two children, Hannah and Land. They endured intense summer heat, winds, dust, cramped quarters and even a degree of danger while accompanying me during much of my research for this book.

Roger Brandt, formerly a ranger at Death Valley National Park, wrote three drives: Cottonwood/Marble canyons, Chloride City and Hole-In-The-Wall. Randy Banis, editor of DeathValley.com, contributed the Wyman Canyon route. Other staffers at Death Valley as well as Joshua Tree National Park, Mojave National Preserve, Red Rock Canyon State Park, Anza-Borrego Desert State Park and Picacho State Recreation Area also provided invaluable assistance.

Many Bureau of Land Management employees contributed generously by suggesting drives, providing information, critiquing parts of the manuscript or verifying information.

I am grateful as well to Dennis Casebier and Friends of the Mojave Road, whose book *Mojave Road Guide: An Adventure Through Time* is an essential companion for anyone considering driving the historic Mojave Road.

Jerry Painter, who produced the maps for each route, has once again made an outstanding contribution.

Publicist Michael Dobrin has long provided the assistance, support and enthusiasm that helped make my *Backcountry Byways* guidebook series possible. I am grateful as well to Toyota Motor Sales, Inc., for providing the comfortable, capable and unfailingly reliable sport-utility vehicles that I've used to research the series, which amounts to the ultimate road test.

Contents

Appendix

Preface

Hiking. Backpacking. Mountain biking. When I was younger, fitter and more foot-loose, I enjoyed them all. But life always seems to make more, not fewer, demands on our time. Thus, over the years work, family and, I must admit, the passing of my physical prime took me away from those once-cherished modes of backcountry travel. As middle age appeared on the horizon, I worried that my days of wandering the wild were over.

Then I discovered that the West's most beautiful and remote regions, occasionally even wilderness areas where mechanized travel is usually prohibited, are crossed by unpaved, often little-known roads. I learned that with a factory-stock sport-utility vehicle, equipped with high clearance and 4-wheel drive, my family and I could have a wildland experience in the comfort and convenience of our family "car" anytime, whether for a few hours or a few days.

Bringing whatever amenities we wanted, we could explore rugged mountain ranges, high plateaus and remote desert canyons by day and then, if we didn't want to camp, relax at a motel at night. A child in diapers? We could carry a case of them. No time to hike? I could drive. That bothersome foot? It would never hold me back again.

I'd broken free of the limitations of time, distance and physical ability. I'd learned that America's most beautiful wildlands were not just for the fit and free, or those who drive motorcycles, ATVs and modified 4x4s. I found most unpaved roads to be easily driveable, while others were rough enough to provide exhilarating moments of adventure and challenge. I didn't need a winch, a lift kit, or oversized tires and wheels.

Over the years, backcountry touring became a bigger and bigger part of my family's outdoor life. With our children, we got to know the beauty and history of the West in ways that would not have been possible for us otherwise.

California Desert Byways, part of my series of backcountry touring guidebooks, will take you along many of the most beautiful and historic unpaved backways in the vast desert region that stretches from Owens Valley to the Mexican border. You will experience the moisture-sapped Sierra rainshadow, remote desert valleys, high mountain crests, slot canyons, cactus gardens, Joshua tree forests, ghost towns, ancient Native American rock art sites and nearly forgotten frontier trails.

Whether you want to get away for a few hours, a day, a weekend or longer, the backcountry byways of the California desert have what you're looking for.

The High Sierra from Mazourka Peak *(Tour 8)*

INTRODUCTION

Titus Canyon *(Tour 13)*

The California Desert
Wasteland or Wonderland?

The desert, vast and still, spread out far to south as I drove down from the Chuckwalla Mountains toward the Bradshaw Trail in remote eastern Riverside County, south of I-10. It was a July afternoon, the time of day and year that gives the desert its fearsome reputation. The landscape, bleached by the high sun, shimmered in the heat. Nothing stirred. I had the place to myself.

I stopped to scan the courses of several spurs. Do I go left? Right? Then the incongruous brilliance of a tiny purple flower caught my eye. Normally, desert flowers bloom in the kinder temperatures and gentler sunshine of spring, after the parched soil has been quenched by winter rains. But here was this delicate little thing, about the size of a quarter, defying punishing heat to bravely bloom in the tenuous shade of an upended stone.

I climbed out of my 4Runner, and admired it up close. It was a reminder that even in summer, when humans in desert country are loathe just to step outside, there is life and beauty in the desert, a place that is simultaneously threatening and inviting, brutal and sublime.

Many of us have long viewed the California desert as a wasteland. To some it has seemed the perfect place to bomb, dump or otherwise destroy for economic, military or recreational purposes. Others have viewed it as a place to be "reclaimed" with water shipped from afar at great financial and environmental cost. But it can seem a wasteland only if one fails to look closely.

Beauty here is subtle and spare. Rainfall averages a scant two to five inches a year. Summer temperatures often soar well above 100° F. Life is pared down to its essentials. Seemingly empty and silent expanses belie the presence of complex and dynamic ecosystems and powerful, active geologic forces. Thus, for many of us, appreciating desert lands is an acquired skill. We scowl at the bleached and sterile face of the desert when the sun is high. But do we notice how that face changes in late afternoon and early evening? Then, when the sun is low, it suffuses the desert with a rich golden hue. Shadows are cast. The texture of every plant, the subtle undulations of the land, the grain of the rocks and the silhouettes of mountain peaks are revealed. In summer, the drab mountains and flats appear monotonous. Yet in spring, after good winter rains, the desert can become a gallery of wildflowers.

As it is typically defined, the California desert reaches from the northern end of Owens Valley to the Mexican border. It encompasses about 25 million acres, extending roughly 400 miles north to south and more than 200 miles east to west at its widest. It is the largest expanse of publicly owned land in the state, and it has been as hot politically as the summer sun. In 1976 Congress established the California Desert Conservation Area, requiring that a comprehensive plan be developed for its protection and management. Then, in 1994, it passed the California Desert Protection Act, adding still more protection. About three million acres are now set aside as military reserves. About 14 million acres have been designated as protected wilderness areas. There are 90 mountain ranges, perhaps more than 100,000 archaeological sites as well as wetlands, waterfalls, lava flows, caverns and gorges. About half a million people call it home.

The desert also is home to plants and animals that have adapted to a life of scarcity. There are bighorn sheep, cougars, tortoises, raptors, cholla cactus gardens and forests of Joshua trees. You'll see roadrunners sprinting along the roadsides. In

Afton Canyon, where the Mojave River provides rare year-round surface water, you might see a soaring eagle in search of a meal. Sometimes, as in the case of the threatened desert tortoise, animals that have for ages endured some of the harshest conditions in North America are now on the brink of extinction.

California's political borders take in three desert environments: the Great Basin, the Mojave Desert, and the Colorado (Sonoran) Desert. From the Great Basin peaks that tower over Owens Valley in the north to the Joshua trees of the Mojave in the middle and the palm oases of the Colorado Desert in the south, the region is a place of contrasts and extremes.

Owens Valley is where the Sierra Nevada, the Great Basin Desert and the Mojave Desert meet. The mountainous, sagebrush-covered Great Basin extends into California from Nevada. It is high desert, mostly 4,000 feet above sea level or higher, and winters are colder there than in the other two deserts. The White Mountains, where White Mountain Peak rises to 14,246 feet, and the Inyo Mountains, a connected range to the south, form the highest range in the Great Basin and the eastern wall of Owens Valley. The valley's western wall is formed by one of the world's steepest escarpments, the eastern side of the Sierra Nevada, the largest and highest single mountain range in the Lower 48. There, the tallest peak in the contiguous states, Mt. Whitney, rises to 14,495 above sea level. Owens Valley itself, called a graben in geologic terms, has subsided and stretched as the mountains flanking it have risen. Today its floor lies some 10,000 feet below the highest peaks flanking it.

The Great Basin lies in the rain shadow of the Sierra. East-flowing Pacific air arrives in the valley sapped of moisture after its journey up the western slope and over the crest of the Sierra. While precipitation on the western slope has averaged as high as 50 inches a year, east of the crest rainfall averages a scant 5 to 15 inches a year. Hence, the White-Inyo Mountains were denied the heavy snows that formed the glaciers that scoured the Sierra. Since the early 1900s, when Los Angeles began appropriating the water that flows down the eastern slope of the Sierra, humans have made that region even drier, even as we've made other desert places bloom through irrigation.

The region extending east from the Sierra to the parched floor of Death Valley is unsurpassed in natural beauty, climatic variety, geologic scale and, importantly, accessibility. In the morning you can leave your piney campsite high above Lone Pine, drive east through the geologic waves of basin and range desert, plunge into Death Valley, head west again through Panamint Valley, and be back at your mountain retreat before sundown.

The Mojave Desert spreads eastward like a fan from the juncture of the Tehachapi Mountains, at the southern tip of the Sierra, and the San Gabriel Mountains. Most of the Mojave is in California. The 1.4-million-acre Mojave National Preserve in the eastern part of the state is its geographic center. Its most recognizable symbol is the Joshua tree, which reminded pioneers of the prophet Joshua's outstretched arms. In the upper Mojave, elevations range between 2,000 and 4,000 feet. In the lower Mojave, Death Valley's 11,049-foot Telescope Peak looms over Badwater Basin; at 282 feet below sea level, Badwater is the lowest point in the western hemisphere.

Joshua Tree National Park occupies the dividing strip between the ecosystems of the Mojave and Colorado deserts. The Colorado Desert encompasses much of southeastern California and most of Sonora in northern Mexico. This is low desert, most of it well below 2,000 feet. Winters are mild. Summers are extremely hot. Bodies of water like the Colorado River, the great canals and aqueducts, and the Salton Sea are peculiar sights indeed.

Human beings have occupied the California desert for tens of thousands of years, and it is common to see evidence of ancient desert dwellers juxtaposed with that of relative newcomers. Sometimes the contrast between what the ancients left behind and what we've been leaving behind for the last century is disturbing. Sometimes it shows how far we've come, how much easier life is for us than it was for our forebears. In other cases it shows how much we have to learn.

For example, at Inscription Canyon near Barstow, a fine place to view ancient rock art, a visitor will notice that Albert Einstein apparently wasn't the first to develop that famous equation after all, for there it is, etched into the desert varnish alongside many mysterious symbols created by Native Americans ages ago. Along the Titus Canyon drive, in Death Valley National Park, you can visit the remains of the mining town of Leadfield, a relic of an attempt by transients to exploit the desert, and the Klare Spring petroglyphs, the art of people for whom the desert was home. Northeast of Barstow, just off the Yellow Brick Road to Las Vegas called Interstate 15, a budding archaeologist can explore the Calico Early Man Site, a prehistoric workshop, quarry and campsite.

The California Desert Protection Act

Human beings and the California desert have been adversaries in many ways for a very long time. But as formidable a foe as the desert has been, we are now in position to decide its fate.

In 1984, a number of conservation groups formed the California Desert Protection League. Its goal was to protect the desert from abuse and destruction by mining, off-highway vehicle use and other activities. In 1986, then-U.S. Sen. Alan Cranston (D-California) sought to further that goal by introducing the California Desert Protection Act. That spurred creation of the California Desert Coalition, an umbrella group of mining interests, ranchers, off-highway vehicle users, some local governments, and others who felt the bill ignored the concerns and interests of traditional desert users and desert residents. They hoped either to kill it, or to minimize its impact.

The legislation didn't pass until October 1994, in the final hours of the 103rd Congress. Passage came only after compromises were reached, and after it became caught up in the hard-fought Senate race between its principal sponsor, U.S. Sen. Dianne Feinstein (D-California), and her Republican challenger, Rep. Michael Huffington. President Bill Clinton signed the bill into law.

It set aside the largest amount of land for wilderness and parks ever in the lower 48 states, adding about 7.7 million acres of new federal wilderness to the 6.3 million acres previously designated in California.

Death Valley National Monument, which encompassed more than two million acres, was made a national park. With the new designation came an additional 1.3 million acres previously managed by the U.S. Bureau of Land Management. Of the park's total acreage, more than 3.1 million are now federally protected wilderness areas. The expansion made it the largest national park in the continental United States, more than a million acres larger than Yellowstone. Its boundaries now take in places like Darwin Falls, a rare year-round desert waterfall, and remote Saline and Eureka valleys, grabens like Owens and Death valleys that are known, respectively, for hot springs and mountainous sand dunes.

Joshua Tree National Monument also became a national park. It was expanded by 234,000 acres, for a total of almost 794,000 acres. Of that, 132,000 acres are now wilderness.

The status of the East Mojave National Scenic Area was upgraded to a 1.4-million-acre national preserve, with 695,000 wilderness acres. Management responsibility was transferred from the BLM to the National Park Service.

The law also created a desert lily preserve, protected dinosaur tracks, added Last Chance Canyon to Red Rock Canyon State Park, and withdrew 6,000 acres adjacent to Bodie State Historic Park from mining and mineral leasing. Some rugged areas are now closed to mechanized travel, yet much of the desert remains open.

Whether one wants more of the region open to four-wheeling, hunting, mining or similar uses, or set aside as places where natural and cultural values will be preserved, the California desert is a treasure that belongs to the nation, not just to Californians, and to future generations, not just to us.

I hope this book enables you to see and appreciate what all the commotion has been about. I hope that you will use the book and your vehicle to experience the desert in a manner that will do no damage and cause no injury to yourself and your passengers. Perhaps you will be able to decide for yourself whether the region is a wasteland, a wonderland, or something in between.

Desert Driving
Backcountry Touring 101

California Desert Byways is intended to introduce backcountry touring to people who travel in factory-stock, high-clearance, four-wheel-drive sport-utility vehicles and pickup trucks equipped for rough off-highway conditions. Since relatively few people who drive such vehicles take advantage of what they can do, I'm going to assume that your experience is limited, and provide some basic know-how. My hope is to help you have a safe and enjoyable experience while protecting the desert's natural environment as well as its historic and cultural sites.

KNOW YOUR VEHICLE. Some automakers, eager to tap into the motoring public's yen for at least the visage of ruggedness, have begun to apply the label "sport-utility" to just about anything with wheels. Don't be fooled. Know what you're driving, and drive within the vehicle's limits as well as your own.

Familiarize yourself with your four-wheel-drive system. Is it a full-time, part-time or automatic system? In a full-time, or permanent, 4WD system, all four wheels are continuously engaged as driving wheels; there is no 2WD mode. (A multimode system, however, will include a 2WD mode.) Full-time 4WD uses either a center differential or viscous coupling to allow the front and rear axles to turn independently for typical daily driving. Some systems allow the driver to "lock" the center differential so that, in poor conditions, both axles will turn together for greater traction. A part-time system uses only the rear wheels as driving wheels until the driver engages 4WD. A part-time system must be disengaged from 4WD on pavement to avoid excessive drivetrain stress. An automatic system is designed to sense on its own when 4WD should be engaged. All-wheel-drive (AWD) systems, such as those used in some passenger cars and vans, provide power to all four wheels much as full-time 4WD systems do. But AWD vehicles are usually designed for all-weather use, not all-terrain use.

Does your vehicle have a transfer case? More than any other single feature, a transfer case identifies a vehicle suited to all-terrain travel. It sends power to the front axles as well as to the rear axles, and, acting as an auxiliary transmission, provides a wider range of gear ratios for a wider range of driving conditions. Use high-range 2WD for everyday driving in normal conditions, both on pavement and off. Use high-range 4WD when added traction is helpful or necessary on loose or slick surfaces, but when conditions are not difficult. Use low-range 4WD in difficult low-speed conditions when maximum traction and power are needed, and to keep engine revs high while moving slowly through rough or steep terrain.

Does the vehicle have all-season highway tires or all-terrain tires? Tires take a terrible beating in off-highway conditions, for which the latter are designed.

Find out where the engine's air intake is, and how high it is. This is important to avoid the devastating consequences of sucking water into the engine through the air intake while fording waterways.

Does the vehicle have steel "skid plates" protecting undercarriage components like the engine oil pan, transfer case and transmission? Skid plates are essential to avoiding the damage that obstacles, particularly roadbed rocks, can inflict.

KNOW WHERE YOU'RE GOING. The maps in this book are general overview maps. For route-finding, you will need a good statewide or regional map in addition to at least one detailed map illustrating the specific area you will be visiting and the route you'll be driving.

For greater detail and navigational purposes, I recommend maps produced by AAA affiliate Automobile Club of Southern California (ACSC), and Bureau of Land Management Desert Access Guides. ACSC maps are outstanding, and are free to AAA members. They often include even the most remote backcountry roads, and I can personally vouch for their accuracy. They are available at AAA travel stores throughout California. BLM Desert Access Guides (there are 31 of them, at $4 each), are available at any BLM office. DAGs used to be user-friendly, stand-alone maps. Unfortunately, they're now combined with the agency's Surface Management Status maps, which are difficult to read and not really designed for the traveling public. However, unlike the old editions, the new DAGs do outline the wilderness areas and parklands that Congress created in 1994 under the California Desert Protection Act. DAGs do cover large areas, show road numbers and are color-keyed to identify public and private lands. They also include information about historic sites, rock art sites, geologic curiosities and other places of interest. They include elevation contours as well. U.S. Geological Survey 7.5-minute topographic maps can be helpful when greater detail is needed, but they don't show road numbers, which are important in the desert, or the new wilderness areas and parklands.

Go over your maps before you begin a drive. Become familiar with sights and landmarks to watch for along the way, and as you travel keep track of your progress so you don't miss important turnoffs, places of interest and worthwhile side trips.

Don't expect to find road signs. The BLM, which has primary responsibility for managing publicly owned tracts of the California desert outside the national and state parks and preserves, does try to keep roads posted, but it's a constant battle with vandals and floods. So pay close attention to your maps and mileages. If you reach a junction where there are several routes to choose from and none has a sign, it's usually best to follow what appears to be the most heavily used route.

Global Positioning System navigation units are increasingly popular. I'm sure some backroad travelers find them handy at times, especially when trying to pinpoint a hard-to-find point of interest, but I've not yet found them necessary.

When venturing into unfamiliar territory, it's sometimes best to rely on road numbers rather than road names, because rural and backcountry roads can have more than one name, or variations of the same name. However, you may find that roads can have more than one numerical designation. Road numbers are changed now and then as well, and a county may assign a number that differs from the number assigned by other agencies to the same road.

WEATHER AND WHEN TO GO.

Elevations vary by thousands of feet in the California desert, resulting in notable climate differences. Generally, the desert travel season is fall through spring, say October or November through April. The mountains, however, get snow in winter, and passes can remain closed well into spring, which seems to be everyone's favorite time to go. Temperatures then are ideal, typically in the 50s at night and 80s during the day. Vegetation is green, the ocotillo, Joshua trees and cacti are in bloom and, if the previous winter has been a wet one, the wildflowers can be startling in their abundance and beauty.

The desert is not the place to be in summer. Temperatures routinely soar into the triple digits, monsoonal downpours cause dangerous flash floods and road washouts, and sand that is dried by summer heat and wind is treacherously soft. The risk of a mishap is higher, the consequences can be far more serious, and since relatively few people venture into the desert in summer, help is much harder to find. Even if you head for the higher and cooler places (much of Death Valley National Park, for example, is thousands of feet above sea level), you will still have to cross the low, sizzling valleys to get there. If you must go in summer, leave your itinerary with someone who isn't going with you, go with at least one other vehicle, and prepare for the worst.

Don't set out on a long drive late in the day, because it's best not to be caught out there after dark unless you've planned an overnight stay.

Pay attention to the sky, even the sky off in the distance, in case a storm is brewing. Stay out of washes and narrow canyons if a storm seems likely. When it rains, desert washes, which often serve as roads, can flood quickly. Dirt roads, when wet, can become dangerously slick and impassable, even with 4WD. Danger aside, driving on muddy roads leaves tracks that can erode into deep ruts.

Since nature has a knack for rudely closing roads without considering our plans, it can be useful to stop at a visitor center or call ahead. Unfortunately, though, finding out the latest road conditions can be difficult. Outside the national parks, visitor centers and ranger stations are often staffed by volunteers who can help with campground locations and such, but who may not know backcountry roads well. To make matters worse, the most knowledgeable individuals at the agencies who manage public lands often are out in the field, not sitting by the telephone or at an information desk. So you may just have to go see for yourself.

GOING ALONE. There is security in having more than one vehicle, and more than one source of ideas and labor if things go awry. It's also fun to be with other people. When you're on vacation, however, or venturing off for a few hours, a day or a weekend, you and yours will probably go alone, in a single vehicle. Now and then, too, an unexpected two-track going off to a canyon or mountain range will unexpectedly catch your eye, and you will succumb to its allure. That's OK, so long as your vehicle is reliable and you're prepared to handle emergencies alone. That said, during certain seasons, particularly spring, you may be surprised by how busy some of these roads can be, for Californians love their backroads, and so do tourists. So while the more remote roads may provide genuine solitude, you may be sharing others with all sorts of users, from mountain bikers, hikers and equestrians to motorcyclists, ranchers and power line workers.

RULES OF THE ROAD. Even in places where no one will be watching, there are rules to follow and practices that help to preserve natural and historic areas. The intent behind them is simple: to keep you safe, to keep your vehicle in good shape, and to protect fragile wildlands and cultural sites from abusive and destructive activities. Misconduct and mistakes can result in personal injury, damage to your vehicle, areas being closed and perhaps even legal penalties.

Here are some things to keep in mind:
- Your vehicle must be street-legal to take these drives. Obey traffic laws and regulatory signs, wear your seat belt, and keep the kids buckled up.
- Drive only on established roads where motor vehicles are permitted. Mechanized travel of any kind, including motorcycles and mountain bikes, is not allowed in designated wilderness areas and wilderness study areas unless a legal corridor exists. Never go "off-road," make a new route, or follow the tracks of someone who did.
- Avoid steep hillsides, stream banks and boggy areas.
- If you get lost or stuck, stay with your vehicle unless you are certain that help is nearby. A vehicle will be much easier for searchers to find than you will be if you've wandered off.
- Some of the places you will visit remain honeycombed with old mines that pose many dangers. View them from a distance.
- Do not touch, collect, remove or in any way disturb such ancient cultural treasures as petroglyphs or geoglyphs. They are protected by federal and state laws.

View them from a distance. Do not use archaeological or historic sites for picnics or camping. The more time people spend at these sites, the greater the likelihood of damage. The same goes for old mines, homesteads, ghost towns and similar sites. Some historic sites, like the ghost town of Cerro Gordo in the Inyo Mountains, are private property. The National Park Service in particular prohibits removing anything at all from lands they manage. In national parks, inquire about backcountry camping and campfire restrictions, such as the prohibition on gathering firewood. On BLM lands, including wilderness, gathering firewood is limited to dead and down materials, but it's best to bring your own wood. The desert has little to spare, and even dead wood is important to desert ecosystems. If you make a fire, keep it small, and use an existing fire ring. If there isn't one, use some kind of metal container or fire pan (a garbage can lid will do) to keep from scorching and blackening the ground. If you go with a group, make only one fire. Haul out your ashes.

- Never camp in washes or narrow canyons, which are subject to flash floods.
- If you camp, remember that the desert doesn't heal as easily as well-watered, forested areas do. Use low-impact practices, and leave no trace of your stay. Use established campsites or areas that show previous use. Bring your own water, and camp at least 300 feet from water sources to avoid damage and pollution, and to allow access by wildlife. Clean up the campsite before you leave, and take your trash with you.
- Leave gates as you find them, i.e. open or closed. Don't disturb livestock.
- Don't drink directly from streams and springs.
- Don't park on grass, sagebrush and the like, because hot exhaust systems can ignite fires.

GO PREPARED. Things can and will go wrong out there, so be prepared to handle problems alone, perhaps even to spend a night or two. On the supplies side, the basics of desert driving are already on the packing list of experienced outdoors enthusiasts: maps, compass, extra eyeglasses and keys, binoculars, trash bags, matches, clothing for inclement weather, hats and sunscreen, blankets or sleeping bags, flashlights and batteries, plenty of food and water (a gallon per person per day is considered the absolute minimum), and something that will make you easy to spot should someone have to come looking for you. Don't forget to augment your supplies with enough non-perishable food and water for a couple of days in case you get stranded.

Here are some more auto-oriented things to bring:

- Topped-off fuel tank. Fill up before every backcountry drive, every time. You will use your vehicle's low gears a lot, which will mean higher fuel consumption than highway driving. It shouldn't be necessary to carry extra fuel. If you do, strap the container to the exterior of the vehicle, preferably the roof. Keep the container full so that dangerous fumes won't build up inside.
- Shovel. Mine has been a life-saver, and is the single most useful tool I carry. Yours will be, too.
- Traction aids. You're going to encounter soft sand, and if you get stuck, your tires are going to need help. Metal "sand ladders," flat lengths of aluminum designed to give tires a firm surface, are available, but a pair of sturdy wooden planks can do the job. Some people carry rolled up strips of heavy carpet, which are compact enough so that you can bring one for each wheel. Whatever you bring, they should be a few inches wider than your tires and about three feet long. Put holes in the ends, and when you use them, connect them with rope to the back of the vehicle. Then, when you drive off, they will follow, and you won't have to walk back to get them.
- Good tires. Smoother tread designs are better in sand, because they tend to float rather than dig down the way aggressive tread patterns do. Be sure you have a good (and properly inflated) spare tire, a jack and a small board to support it on dirt. Also bring a couple of cans of pressurized tire sealant (available at department stores); a small electric air compressor (the kind that plugs into the cigarette lighter) so you can get the tires back up to proper pressure after airing down for sand; and a tire pressure gauge. A warning: Old mine sites and ghost towns are often littered with nails and broken glass.
- Some basic tools, including jumper cables, duct tape, electrical tape, baling wire, spare fuses, multipurpose knife, high-strength tow strap, fire extinguisher, and a plastic sheet to put on the ground when making repairs. An assortment of screws, washers, nuts and such could come in handy as well, especially if you're driving an older or modified (meaning trouble-prone) vehicle.

I keep much of this stuff ready to go in a large plastic storage container. It's also important to tie it all down so it doesn't get tossed about on rough terrain.

Sometimes I bring my mountain bike as a backup vehicle. Since I do a lot of exploring, I also use it to check out places that I don't want to drive to. Consider getting a CB radio and roof antenna, even though transmitting range is limited. These days, a cellular telephone can be handy, although they often don't work in the wild.

OFF-HIGHWAY DRIVING. Most of the time, simply driving more slowly and cautiously than you do on paved roads will get you where you want to go and back again. Here are some tips for those inevitable times when the going will get rough.

All thumbs? You won't be for long if you forget to keep them on top of the steering wheel. Otherwise, the wheel's spokes can badly injure your thumbs if a front wheel is suddenly jerked in an unexpected direction. If the steering wheel is being rocked back and forth by the terrain, keep your hands loose on the wheel, at 10 and 2 o'clock.

Lean forward in especially rough conditions, keeping your back away from the seat, and you won't be tossed about so much.

Uphill traffic has the right of way, if practical, because it's usually easier and safer to back up to a pullout, using gravity as a brake, than to back down a slope while fighting the pull of gravity.

Think ahead. If you have a part-time 4WD system, engage it before you need it to stay out of trouble.

When in doubt, scout. If you're uncertain about the road ahead, check it out on foot..

Air down in sand, deep mud and rocky terrain. While standard tire pressure usually will provide adequate traction, deep mud and soft, dry sand require temporarily airing down (letting air out) to 15 psi or perhaps even 10 psi to expand the tire's "footprint" for greater flotation. The risk in doing this, however, is that you will lose ground clearance and the tires' sidewalls will bulge, making them more vulnerable to cuts and punctures.

On rocky terrain, airing down to perhaps 20 psi will soften the ride and lessen the punishment the roadbed inflicts on the suspension. On especially rocky and steep ground, airing down also will allow the tires to wrap themselves around the rocks for better grip. Shallow mud can be underlain by firm ground, so normal tire inflation or over-inflation can help tires penetrate to terra firma.

Remember to re-inflate the tires before driving at speed or on pavement.

Maintain speed and forward momentum. Go as slow as you can, but as fast as you must. Slowing down or stopping in sand and mud can be the worst thing to do. Keep up your speed, and keep moving. Drive in established tracks. Higher gears tend to be more effective in poor-traction conditions than lower gears.

Because of the range of problems that driving in mud poses (roadbed damage, vehicle damage, transporting biological organisms from one ecosystem to another), avoid it. If it rains, pull onto firm, high ground and let the storm pass. Then wait for the road to dry out and for any potential flood danger to pass.

If you begin to lose traction in mud, turn the steering wheel rapidly one way and then the other, back and forth. That can help the tires grip. If you do get stuck, dig out the sides of the tires to relieve suction, and pack debris around the tires for traction.

Dust storms and flash floods are dangerous. Blinding dust storms can kick up suddenly in the desert. Do not attempt to drive through one. Instead, pull over to a safe place, turn off the engine and wait it out, keeping windows and doors closed.

In summer, the season of sudden monsoonal downpours, you are likely to encounter floods and washed-out roads. Never enter a flooded area. If you're in a wash or narrow canyon when a storm appears to be developing, even far away, get out, or at least get to high ground. If a section of road is washed out, you'll have to decide for yourself whether you can get through safely. Often, though, desert floods will create steep and high banks and debris fields that you won't be able to get over or through, at least not easily.

Stick to the high points. When the going gets particularly rough, shift into low range, go slow, and keep the tires on the high spots, thus keeping the undercarriage high and away from obstacles that can damage the differentials, or so-called "pumpkins," or other components. Place the tires on the rocks to keep the vehicle high. Do not let large rocks pass directly beneath the vehicle.

Straddle ruts, letting them pass beneath the vehicle. If you must cross a rut, do so at an angle, easing one tire at a time across it. Do the same for depressions, dips, ledges or "steps," and ditches.

If you get stuck, don't panic. Calmly analyze the situation, and with thought and work, you'll get out. Don't spin your tires, which will dig you in deeper. Jack up the vehicle if you can, backfill the hole beneath the problem wheel, building a base high enough to give you a bit of a rolling downhill start. Put the planks, sand ladders or strips of carpet you brought beneath and ahead of each tire (or behind, if you're hoping to back out) for traction. If you have water to spare, dampen the sand to firm it up. Lower the vehicle, and if you're faced with soft sand, lower the tire pressure to 10-15 psi to increase the tires' footprint.

If the vehicle gets high-centered, meaning your undercarriage is lodged on something and your tires can't grip the ground, take out your jack (don't use a bumper jack) and the little board you brought to set it on. Carefully raise the vehicle, little by little, placing rocks, dirt and debris under each suspended tire until you've made a downslope that will help you get going and keep going.

To get over a ledge, either use the rock ramp that is likely to be there already, or use a few nearby rocks to build one. Put one wheel over at a time. Don't leave an excavation site behind.

Be prepared to remove deadfall from the roadway. Occasionally you may encounter a fallen tree or limb in the road. It's usually possible to drive around it. If you must drive over it, approach at an angle and put one wheel at a time over it. If you carry a folding saw, as I do, cut it away. If the obstacle is too large to cut or move by hand, consider using your tow strap to pull it out of the way.

Have someone act as a spotter to help you maneuver through difficult places, and use low range and a low gear for better control.

Try not to spin your tires, which tears up the road and can get you stuck, or stuck worse than you already may be. Some newer 4WD vehicles have sophisticated electronic traction-control systems designed to eliminate wheel spin by instantly transferring power from spinning wheels to the wheel or wheels with traction. Some Toyota SUVs and trucks can be purchased with locking differentials, a.k.a. "lockers." These mechanisms vastly improve your ability to get through or out of nasty off-highway situations by equalizing power to the driving wheels and eliminating the differential's tendency to transfer power to the wheel with the least traction. I recommend them.

Hills are often badly chewed up by the spinning tires of vehicles that lack locking differentials or traction control systems. If you encounter such a hill, shift into low range and keep your wheels on the high spots between the holes.

Before climbing over a steep, blind hilltop, find out what's up there and on the other side. Depending on how steep it is and how much power your vehicle has, shift into low range. Drive straight up, accelerate as you climb, keep moving, then slow down as you near the top.

If the engine stalls on a hill, stop and immediately set the parking brake hard and tight. Here, an automatic transmission can help you get going again easily. Just shift into "park" and turn the key. If you have a manual transmission, you may be able to compression-start the engine if you're facing downhill. If you're facing uphill, try shifting into first gear/low range. Turn the engine over without clutching, and let the starter motor move things along a bit until the engine starts and takes over. Otherwise, you'll have to work the clutch, hand brake and accelerator simultaneously to get going again without rolling backward. Modern clutch-equipped vehicles require the driver to depress the clutch pedal to start the engine, which is fine in a parking lot but difficult on a steep mountain incline. However, some vehicles have clutch bypass switches that let you start the engine without depressing the clutch, a great help when stalled on a climb.

If you can't make it up a hill, don't try to turn around. Stop, and put the transmission in reverse/low range. Tilt the exterior mirrors, if you can, so that you can see what the rear tires are doing. Then slowly back straight down. Never descend in neutral, relying on the brakes. If you must apply the brakes, do so lightly and steadily to minimize the risk of losing traction and going into a slide. Go straight down steep inclines, using low range and the lowest driving gear so the engine can help brake. But remember that automatic transmissions, which I think are best overall, don't provide as much engine-braking ability as manual transmissions.

Avoid traversing the side of a steep hill. Occasionally, though, mountain roads do cross steep slopes, sometimes tilting the vehicle "off-camber," or toward the downhill side. It's almost always an unnerving experience for me. Lean heavily (no pun intended) toward caution under such circumstances. You might want to remove cargo from the roof to lower your vehicle's already-high center of gravity. Then go slow. It might help to turn the front wheels up-slope, into the hill. If you decide not to continue, do not attempt to turn around. Tilt the exterior mirrors so you can watch the rear tires, shift into reverse/low range for greater low-speed control, and slowly back up until you reach a spot where you can turn around safely.

Don't cross waterways if there's an alternative. Fording streams and shallow rivers is fun, to be sure. But many living things reside in or otherwise depend on streams, and can be harmed by careless and unnecessary crossings that stir up sediment and erode stream banks. If you must cross, use an established crossing point. Check the depth with a stick if necessary, comparing the depth to your vehicle (hub deep generally is the deepest you should go). Or walk across first. Don't cross if the current is fast and deep. Never enter a desert wash if it's flooding. Often, a somewhat fast-moving perennial stream will be safer to cross than a sluggish one, because continuously moving water prevents sediments from settling, keeping the bed rocky and firm. Slow-moving or still water, on the other hand, lets sediment and mud build up.

Once across, stop and inspect the vehicle. The brakes will be wet, so use them a few times to dry them out. The tires also will be wet, and may not grip the roadbed as well.

ACCESSORIES AND SUCH. Properly equipped, even stock 4WD SUVs and pickups are built to take people to places that sedans, vans and station wagons either cannot go, or shouldn't. Despite their comforts, they are rugged and reliable transport—backcountry or frontcountry. They can go from the showroom straight into the hills without modifications.

One of my family's two Toyota 4Runners has a 5-speed manual transmission and a stock 4-cylinder engine, which I've found to be adequate even when it's loaded with the four of us and our camping gear. The other has a relatively fuel-frugal V6 and automatic transmission. I've never felt any need for a large, thirsty V8.

Manual transmissions can require three feet: one for the brake, one for the clutch and one for the accelerator, all working pretty much simultaneously. So I prefer automatic transmissions, which I find much easier to use in the rough.

I've learned to appreciate options that I once dismissed as unnecessary. Easily adjusted electric side mirrors, for example, will pay for themselves the first time you have to back up a narrow shelf road with a killer drop-off. When I'm exploring narrow, high-walled canyons, a sunroof/moonroof is a handy option indeed.

There is a huge four-wheel-drive accessories market. Are those add-ons necessary? It depends on how much, and what type, of adventure motoring you plan to do. The requirements of serious four-wheeling on technically challenging routes differ from those of backcountry touring. Technically challenging routes can require extensive vehicle modifications that may degrade on-highway performance and reliability. On most backcountry roads, however, a stock vehicle will do fine. If you enjoy traveling the West's vast network of backcountry roads, you never know what you might encounter, so there can be real benefits to adding extra lights, beefier tires, a more versatile roof carrier, heavier skid plates, perhaps even an after-market locking differential. (I've never owned a winch.)

Maintenance is essential. Backcountry roads are hard on vehicles, so follow the recommendations in your owner's manual for dusty, wet and muddy conditions. Check the tires often, because no part of your vehicle will take a greater beating. If you pass through an old mining area, expect to pick up a nail now and then.

FAMILY FUN. Backcountry roads provide terrific opportunities to explore wildlands easily and conveniently, but trying to keep kids happy on car trips has always been tough. Still, there are things you can do to make touring the backcountry fun for them.

- Don't just drive. Stop, and stop often. Watch for wildlife, especially early in the morning or evening. Visit historic and prehistoric sites like ghost towns and rock-art sites.
- Pick up a book or two that will help you identify, understand and explain the region's history, scenery, vegetation and wildlife. Looking up the story behind place names can be fun.
- Make a photocopy of the area on the map where you'll be going. Let the kids help you navigate and identify peaks, creeks, historic sites and other landmarks.
- Bring at least one personal cassette or CD player (the latter will need good anti-shock protection so that playback is not affected by bumps). If you have small children, check out some children's cassette tapes or CDs from your public library. They've been lifesavers for my family on many long trips. Audio books, which I listen to myself on long drives, are great diversions for children as well. Many video rental stores carry them.
- Bring an inexpensive point-and-shoot camera and binoculars for the kids to use.
- If you have a licensed teenage driver on board, let him or her drive now and then. The sooner a teen learns backcountry driving skills, the longer he or she will remain an eager participant. And someday you may need a capable co-pilot.
- Bring snacks, preferably the non-sticky kind, and drinks. There will be plenty of bumps on your adventures, so cups with spill-proof tops are essential. Plastic garbage bags, paper towels, changes of clothing, wet wipes and pillows are also good to have along.

Make the drive part of a day that draws on the huge range of experience the California desert has to offer. Plan a picnic. Hike to a hilltop. Ride your mountain bikes. And do something civilized when you get back to town: Go out to dinner.

PRESERVE THE PRIVILEGE. If you're particularly interested in helping to preserve opportunities to travel responsibly through public lands, contact Tread Lightly!, Inc., a non-profit organization founded to promote responsible use of off-highway vehicles. It is based in Ogden, Utah. Call 1-800-966-9900.

As you travel, tell me what you've found, whether you've found mistakes, or have trips and tips you'd like to see added to future editions. Write to me in care of Wilderness Press, 1200 Fifth St., Berkeley, CA 94710.

How to Use
California Desert Byways

LOCATION: Where the drive is.

HIGHLIGHTS: An overview of the appealing elements of the drive. (The icons accompanying each route suggest additional attractions.)

DIFFICULTY: I assume you are not a serious four-wheeler, but someone in a stock, high-clearance 4-wheel-drive (4WD) vehicle with all-terrain tires and a transfer case with high and low range. That said, the ratings are: *easy*, which means it probably won't require 4WD unless conditions deteriorate; *moderate*, which means slower going in 4WD, with rough spots, rocks, sand, deep ruts, etc., but little or no technical terrain; and *difficult*, which means some technical four-wheeling, rough and slow going, and the possibility of vehicle damage.

TIME & DISTANCE: The approximate time it takes to complete the drive, and the distance you will travel.

MAPS: Each description includes an overview map, with the road highlighted. Scale is approximate. For route-finding, use at least one of the maps that I cite here. I primarily recommend Automobile Club of Southern California (ACSC) maps, U.S. Bureau of Land Management (BLM) Desert Access Guides, and U.S. Forest Service (USFS) maps. Occasionally, I recommend U.S. Geological Survey (USGS) topographic maps, topo maps produced by National Geographic Maps/Trails Illustrated, and various other readily available maps. Sometimes I also cite a useful supplementary publication. You can obtain these materials from outdoor recreation equipment retailers, book and map retailers, AAA offices, BLM offices and Wilderness Press.

INFORMATION: A source for road conditions and other information. Telephone numbers, addresses and Web sites (current at the time of publication) are listed at the back of the book.

GETTING THERE: How to reach the starting point. I typically describe routes going in a particular direction to help you locate and identify landmarks. Many drives can be taken in the opposite direction.

REST STOPS: Picnic areas, campgrounds, historic sites, etc.

THE DRIVE: Here I provide details such as historical background, points of interest, where to turn, odometer readings and such.

Map Symbols

Point of interest	■	Information	?
Paved road	▬▬▬	Hiking trail	- - ⌒ - - -
Easy dirt road	≈≈≈	Forest or county road	3S01
Primitive road	≈ ≈ = = ∕	Interstate highway	5
Camping	▲	U.S. highway	101
Lake	⬤	State highway	1
Waterway	∼∼∼	North indicator	↑ N
Mountain	⌒⌒		
Ranger station	⚑		
Picnic area	⊼		
City or town	○		

Tours in shaded background

Paved road

Easy dirt road

Primitive road

Guide To Tour Highlight Icons

Mountain biking

Wildlife viewing

Photo opportunities

Camping

Hiking

Historic sites

Rock Art

Picnicking

Restaurant

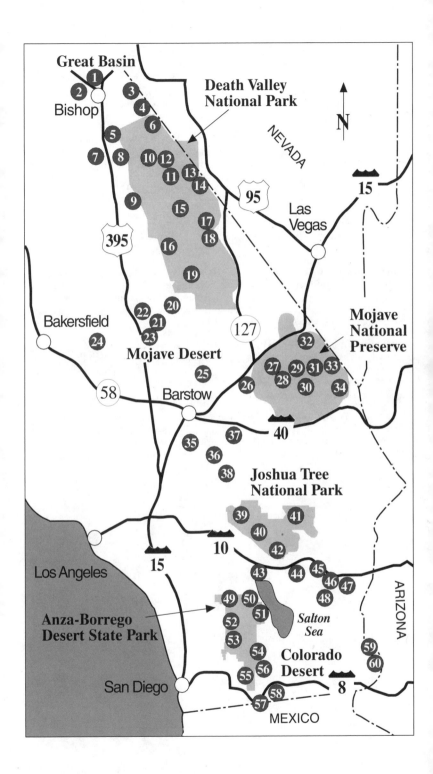

Author's Favorites

Inyo Mountains (Tour 8)—The views of the Sierra Nevada, Owens Valley, the basin and range country to the east and the Inyos themselves are truly breathtaking. Add to that the adrenaline of a few spots that can be a bit challenging, and you have a nearly perfect backcountry drive.

Saline Valley Road (Tour 10)—This is one of three outstanding alternate routes for touring Death Valley National Park. Like the Owens Valley to Death Valley Road (Tour 6), it rises and falls through the waves of basin and range country as it takes you down into remote Saline Valley and vast Panamint Valley. You can add the Hidden Valley and Racetrack Valley Road tours (11 and 12) as well. The clothing-optional hot springs along the way certainly add interest.

Last Chance Canyon (Tour 22)—Colorful cliffs, narrow canyon washes and a long and colorful human history make the Last Chance Canyon area particularly interesting and scenic.

Jawbone to Lake Isabella (Tour 24)—The views are inspiring indeed as you climb up the eastern side of the Sierra, making the transition from the Mojave Desert to conifer forests. Pastoral Kelso Valley is reminiscent of old California. Then, as you descend down switchbacks toward the lake, you are greeted with even more terrific views.

Augustine Pass (Tour 47)—The Chuckwalla Mountains, now largely legally designated wilderness, are impressive from a distance. To drive through them on this tiny single-lane road, which winds through a narrow, steep-walled canyon, gives you an even greater appreciation for their complexity and beauty. The appeal of this route is enhanced by its link to the historic Bradshaw Trail (Tour 48).

Fish Creek Wash (Tour 54)—If you only have time for one drive in Anza-Borrego Desert State Park, this is the one to take. The varied scenery is outstanding. Highlights include Split Mountain, with its strange anticline (layered rock bent by enormous geologic pressure), wind caves and narrow, high-walled Sandstone Canyon.

THE DRIVES

Volcanic Tableland

LOCATION: North of Bishop in Mono and Inyo counties, between U.S. 395 & U.S. 6.

HIGHLIGHTS: The Volcanic Tableland formed 700,000 years ago when vents of the Long Valley Caldera, to the northwest, spewed clouds of hot rhyolitic ash and rock. It includes petroglyphs, Red Rock Canyon and views of the Sierra and the White Mountains. Early on, the route passes through the Fish Slough Area of Critical Environmental Concern, a 36,000-acre area of wetlands, alkali meadows and uplands where the Mojave Desert and Great Basin meet.

DIFFICULTY: Easy to moderate.

TIME & DISTANCE: 52 miles; 3 hours.

MAP: Inyo National Forest. Follow it closely.

INFORMATION: BLM's Bishop Field Office.

GETTING THERE: In Bishop, take U.S. 6 north for 1.4 miles. Where it bends east, go left onto Five Bridges Road. Drive 2.4 miles. After passing through a gravel yard and crossing a canal, go right (north) onto Fish Slough Road (3V01).

REST STOPS: There are no services or facilities. Do not touch or disturb the petroglyphs. Overnight visitors should use the BLM's year-round Climbers' Winter Campground or the Horton Creek or Pleasant Valley campgrounds.

THE DRIVE: Fish Slough Road passes the only natural springs remaining on the floor of Owens Valley. 6.7 miles from where you turned onto it is the first petroglyph site, where you can also see grinding holes. The next site is 4 miles farther north, behind a fence on the right after you drop into Chidago Canyon. The best site is another 5.6 miles north, among the rocks to the left (west). A half-mile north of there, go left (west) onto Chidago Canyon Road (3S53), to Red Rock Canyon. After 3S53 exits the canyon and passes Morris Mine Road, it reaches a junction. 3S53, or "Chidago Loop" as a sign might state, bends right (east). Go straight, taking 4S34 for 2.5 miles, then turn left (east) onto little 4S41. About 1.1 mile farther, after climbing high into the piney desert hills, you'll be facing east toward the White Mountains. 4S41 goes right (south) here. In 2.8 miles it comes to a rough downhill section with a stunning view of the Sierra. Once down it, go left (south) 0.4 mile to the small track leading to Casa Diablo Mine, an early-20th century gold mine. A short distance to the right is graded Casa Diablo Mine Road (shown on the Inyo forest map as both 3S02 and 4S04). You can take it southeast for 19 miles to Bishop. I suggest taking 3S02 north for 6.7 miles to Benton Crossing Road (2S84). Turn left (west) there. At Waterson Divide turn south onto Owens Gorge Road (4S02), which will deliver you to U.S. 395 at Tom's Place.

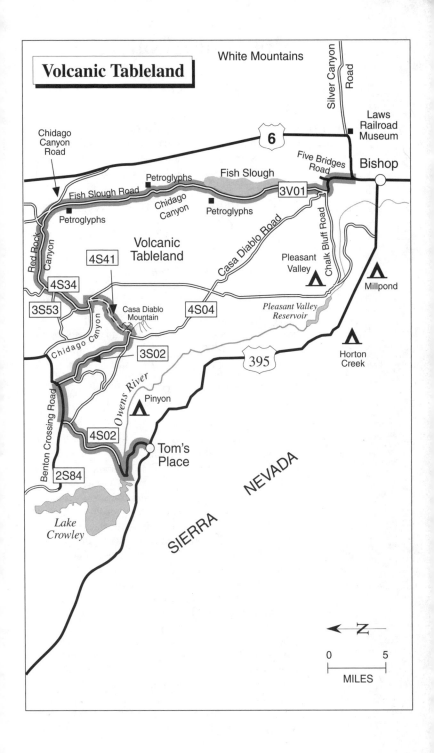

Volcanic Tableland

Buttermilk Country

LOCATION: West of Bishop. Inyo County.

HIGHLIGHTS: The Sierra Nevada is the highest and largest mountain range in the Lower 48. On the east flank one experiences the drying effect the range has on Pacific air currents as they move into the Great Basin. The views stretch from peaks more than 13,000 feet high across 10,000-foot-deep Owens Valley to the Great Basin's White Mountains.

DIFFICULTY: Easy to moderate. Spurs are moderate to difficult.

TIME & DISTANCE: This is a 15-mile loop, or longer if you explore the many spurs. Allow 1.5-2 hours.

MAPS: Inyo National Forest. ACSC's *Eastern Sierra*.

INFORMATION: Inyo NF, White Mt. Ranger Station.

GETTING THERE: In Bishop, go west from U.S. 395 (Main St.) onto West Line St. (Hwy. 168). In 7.3 miles, just into the national forest, go right onto Buttermilk Road (7S01).

REST STOPS: There are many places to stop, including primitive campsites. There are campgrounds south of Buttermilk Country as well. Bishop has all services.

THE DRIVE: I've heard two reasons for the name Buttermilk Country. One says teamsters from a sawmill on Birch Creek long ago would stop for a drink of buttermilk at a dairy. Another says that when 19th-century ranchers would haul goat milk to Bishop in the summer months, it would turn to buttermilk along the way. Today, visitors get to drink in pure scenic grandeur. About 4 miles from Hwy. 168, after you pass through Los Angeles-owned Longley Meadow, Buttermilk Road diminishes to a single lane, and becomes rougher as it angles southwest and takes you gradually higher. If you've never felt dwarfed by nature before, this should do it, for you are driving below the ramparts of such sentinels as Mt. Tom (13,652 feet), Basin Mountain (13,181 feet), Mt. Humphreys (13,986 feet) and Mt. Emerson (13,118 feet), which do their part to sap Pacific air currents of moisture and create the Sierra's semi-arid rainshadow. Soon the road turns south behind Grouse Mountain. Then it's on through a stand of pines and aspens, a change from the vast expanses of sage-covered high desert. The road crosses McGee Creek, then makes a steep but short climb out of the creek's ravine. A rocky but worthwhile 4x4 spur, 8S17, branches to the right, and climbs to a basin in about a mile. Beyond this spur, Buttermilk Road crosses Birch Creek, then turns away from the mountains and begins the gradual descent along a narrow ridge overlooking Hwy. 168 and Bishop Creek Canyon, and soon brings you to the highway and tour's end.

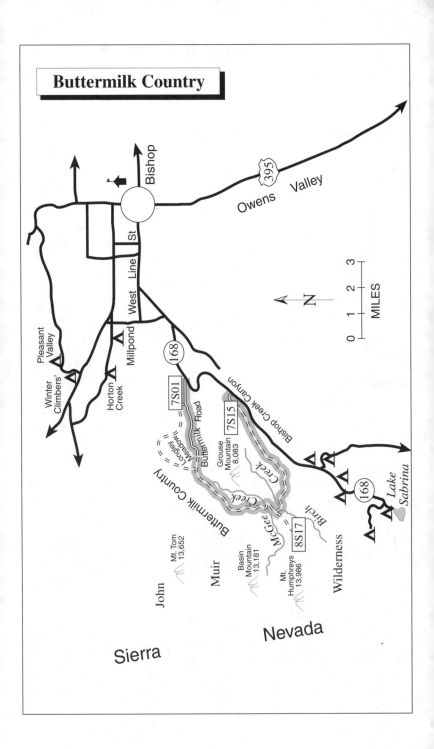

Buttermilk Country

White Mountains

LOCATION: Inyo National Forest, east of Bishop. Mono and Inyo counties.

HIGHLIGHTS: Explore California's second-highest range while climbing to about 11,680 feet. Between the Sierra Nevada and the Whites is 10,000-foot-deep Owens Valley. The Whites are noted for bristlecone pines that are more than 4,600 years old. The drive links up with Wyman Canyon (Tour 4).

DIFFICULTY: The roads atop the Whites are easy gravel. I rate the upper 3.9 miles of Silver Canyon Road (6S02) moderate going uphill. It's steep and narrow with tight switchbacks. The lower 6.5 miles are easy. It's best to go down, because the driving is easier and you can enjoy views of the canyon, Owens Valley, and the Sierra. White Mountain Road from Hwy. 168 to Schulman Grove is paved.

TIME & DISTANCE: All day; about 68 miles from U.S. 395 at Big Pine to U.S. 395 at Bishop. The hike to White Mountain Peak is a strenuous, 15-mile (round-trip) trek from the locked gate at the north end of the drive.

MAPS: Inyo National Forest. ACSC's *Eastern Sierra.*

INFORMATION: Inyo National Forest, White Mountain Ranger Station. The visitor center at Schulman Grove.

GETTING THERE: From Big Pine (eventually going down Silver Canyon Road): Go northeast on Hwy. 168 toward Westgard Pass. 12.7 miles from Big Pine, turn north on White Mountain Road. **From Bishop** (going up Silver Canyon Road)**:** About 3.8 miles northeast of town on U.S. Hwy. 6, go east on Silver Canyon Road (6S02). The gates on the roads leading into the White Mountains are closed in winter.

REST STOPS: No water, fuel or services are available. Grandview Campground is 5.4 miles north of Hwy. 168 on White Mountain Road. Schulman Grove has the oldest known bristlecones, a visitor center, trails and a picnic area. Patriarch Grove has the largest known bristlecone, and picnic tables.

THE DRIVE: The White Mountains and the Sierra were formed simultaneously, but are geologically, climatically and visually distinct. The well-watered and forested Sierra is generally glaciated granite, an igneous rock. The Whites are primarily sedimentary rock 500 million to 600 million years old. While fossils are scarce in the Sierra, fossils nearly 600 million years old are found here. Standing in the rain shadow of the Sierra, these mountains lack the precipitation that formed glaciers in the Sierra. They appear barren but for the hardy, gnarled bristlecones. The Ancient Bristlecone Scenic Byway winds through the Whites' rocky mountaintops. It ends at a locked gate at the north end, at about 11,680 feet. Hikers climb from there to White Mountain Peak, California's third-highest at 14,246 feet.

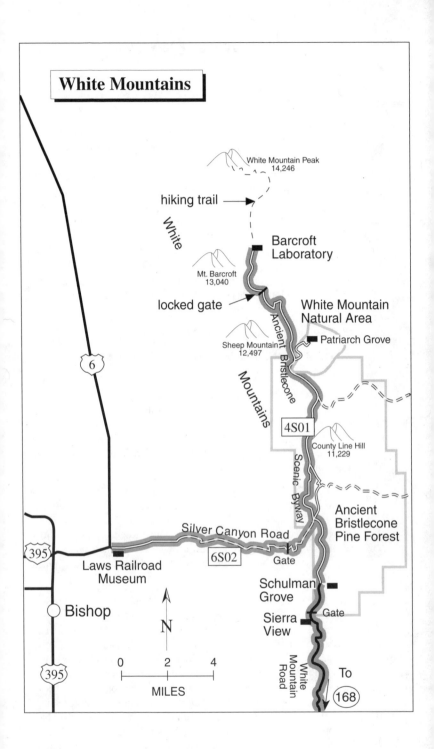

White Mountains

White Mountain Peak
14,246

hiking trail →

White

Barcroft
Laboratory

Mt. Barcroft
13,040

locked gate →

White Mountain
Natural Area

Ancient Bristlecone

Sheep Mountain
12,497

Patriarch Grove

Mountains

4S01

County Line Hill
11,229

Scenic Byway

Ancient
Bristlecone
Pine Forest

Silver Canyon Road

6S02

Gate

Laws Railroad
Museum

Schulman
Grove

Gate

Bishop

Sierra
View

White Mountain Road

To

168

N

0   2   4

MILES

Wyman Canyon

LOCATION: North of Hwy. 168, on the east side of the White Mountains northeast of Big Pine. Inyo National Forest. Inyo County.

HIGHLIGHTS: You will ascend the Great Basin's highest mountains, famous for ancient bristlecone pines, by following meandering Wyman Creek up a beautiful canyon where the vegetation—pinyon pines, wildflowers and meadows—can be quite verdant. At the bottom are the remains of White Mountain City, an 1860s center for processing silver ore from nearby mines. On the crest of the Whites you will link up with the White Mountains tour (No. 3). You can descend to Bishop via spectacular Silver Canyon if you wish.

DIFFICULTY: Moderate.

TIME & DISTANCE: 3 hours; 16 miles. However, getting to the starting point, exploring the White Mountains further and then driving down makes for a full day.

MAPS: Inyo National Forest. ACSC's *Eastern Sierra.*

INFORMATION: Inyo National Forest, White Mountain Ranger Station.

GETTING THERE: From Big Pine, on U.S. 395, take Hwy. 168 across Westgard Pass into Deep Springs Valley. After 27.5 miles, turn left at the Deep Springs Maintenance Station, onto a dirt road. Follow it north 1.3 miles to road 6S01. Then go left toward the site of White Mountain City. The gates on the roads leading into the White Mountains are closed in winter.

REST STOPS: Camping is not permitted in the BLM's 640-acre White Mountain City Area of Critical Environmental Concern. No water, fuel or services are available. Grandview Campground is 5.4 miles north of Hwy. 168 on White Mountain Road. Schulman Grove has the oldest known bristlecones, a visitor center, trails and a picnic area. Patriarch Grove has the largest known bristlecone, and picnic tables.

THE DRIVE: Almost the entire length of Wyman Creek Road (6S01) follows a power line that carries electricity from Owens Valley to several Nevada communities. About 2 miles from Hwy. 168 are the ruins of White Mountain City, which was once involved in an election scandal that resulted from many more votes being cast than there were residents in the precinct. A mile beyond the ruins, in the national forest, the road climbs left, out of the streambed and across open flats for nearly 5 miles. It then re-enters the streambed, making numerous crossings as you pass through pinyon-pine forest for several miles. You will pass the fork to Roberts Ranch, and about 2 miles farther enter the Ancient Bristlecone Pine Forest. The road climbs for another 4 miles, to a fork. Either choice will take you to the main road along the crest. To take Silver Canyon Road (6S02) down to Bishop, take the left fork.

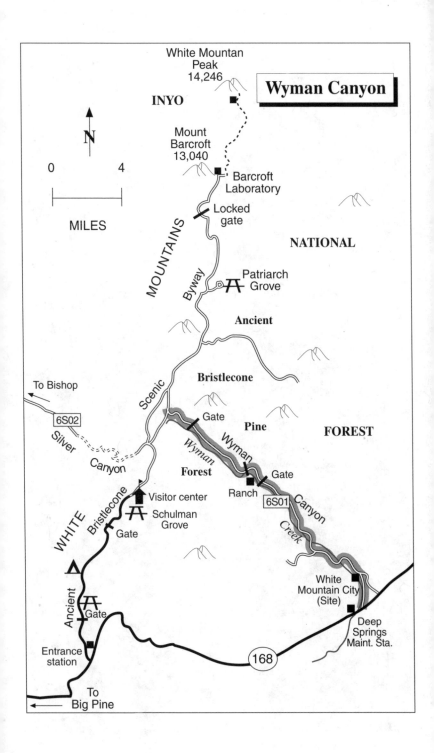

Petroglyphs, volcanic tableland *(Tour 1)*

Natural Arch, Papoose Flat *(Tours 5 & 8)*

The Narrows—Papoose Flat

LOCATION: Inyo Mountains, southeast of Big Pine. Inyo County.

HIGHLIGHTS: This loop winds along a narrow canyon bottom to an even narrower high-walled cleft, The Narrows. It continues to Papoose Flat, a high expanse marked by countless large granite outcrops (including one with an arch) and terrific views across Owens Valley to the High Sierra. At Papoose Flat it connects with Tour 8, Inyo Mountains.

DIFFICULTY: Easy. The canyon bottom is rocky and sandy in places. This is a well-marked route.

TIME & DISTANCE: 3.5 hours; 25.5 miles.

MAP: Inyo National Forest.

INFORMATION: Inyo NF's Mt. Whitney Ranger Station.

GETTING THERE: Take Hwy. 168 east from U.S. 395 at Big Pine. In 2.2 miles turn right (southeast) onto paved Death Valley Road (a.k.a. Saline Valley Road and Big Pine to Death Valley Road). In another 11.2 miles turn right (south) at the sign for Papoose Flat. In 0.1 mile you will come to a Y, the start of the loop. Set your odometer to 0. From here you can go in either direction. The left branch (9S14, the way I describe) follows a long canyon to The Narrows, then continues to Papoose Flat. The southbound branch (9S15) goes first to Papoose Flat.

REST STOPS: There are primitive campsites at various locations.

THE DRIVE: From the Y at the start, the left (eastward) branch (9S14) follows the bottom of a long, rocky ravine. It climbs for about 3.7 miles to a divide, then descends to a narrow canyon. About 3 miles from the divide, at a left spur marked by old mine buildings, is the entrance to The Narrows, a high-walled gap of dark, laminated rock (schist). From there the road becomes 10S07 as it continues south to Squaw Flat along the Inyo Mountains Wilderness. 2 miles from The Narrows is a 4-way junction; go left (right, if you're going in the opposite direction). In a mile, where 9S14 branches left, keep right. Soon you will enter an area of large granite boulders. Papoose Flat, a food-gathering place for Indians for thousands of years, is ahead. Watch for a large rock island just north of the road where erosion has formed an arch. Less than a mile farther is road 9S15, a 4WD road that climbs south to Badger Flat, on the Inyo Mountains tour. Gaze at the Sierra, then go right (north), then right again at the small Y. The road crosses Papoose Flat, then descends to the Y at the start of the loop. If you go in the opposite direction at the outset, the southbound (right) branch (9S15) climbs to Papoose Flat, where you'll go left (east) on 10S07 to The Narrows.

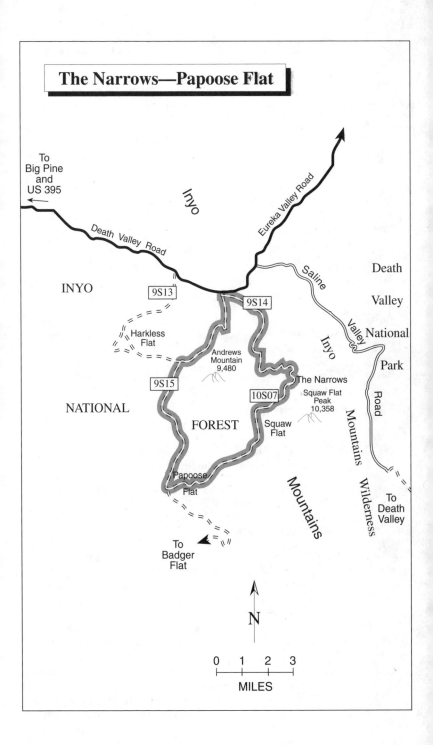

The Narrows—Papoose Flat

Owens Valley—Death Valley

LOCATION: Between Big Pine, on U.S. 395, and the Grapevine Ranger Station in northeastern Death Valley National Park. Inyo County.

HIGHLIGHTS: You will travel from 10,000-foot deep Owens Valley, at the base of the Sierra, through the Inyo Mountains, then plunge into Eureka Valley, in the remote, forbidding yet magnificent northern reaches of Death Valley National Park. Along the way is a side trip to 700-foot-high Eureka Dunes, the highest sand dunes in the Great Basin. Then you will cross the Last Chance Range. The trip ends near volcanic Ubehebe Crater, just north of the Grapevine Ranger Station and that odd Moorish-style edifice, Scotty's Castle.

DIFFICULTY: Easy, on a serpentine 2WD road, much of which is paved. Expect extreme heat in summer, when flash floods can close the road. Snow can temporarily close the road through the Inyo Mountains in winter.

TIME & DISTANCE: 5-6 hours; almost 93 miles with the side trip to Eureka Dunes.

MAPS: ACSC's *Guide to Death Valley*, or Trails Illustrated's *Death Valley National Park* topo map (No. 221).

INFORMATION: Death Valley National Park. Eastern Sierra InterAgency Visitor Center at Lone Pine.

GETTING THERE: From Big Pine, drive east on Hwy. 168 for 2.2 miles. Turn right (southeast) onto Big Pine-Death Valley Road.

REST STOPS: Eureka Dunes has primitive, waterless campsites. Otherwise, there are no services along the drive. Scotty's Castle has food, fuel and water. Developed Mesquite Spring campground is near Scotty's Castle.

THE DRIVE: The paved road from Hwy. 168 over the Inyo Mountains will take you through the narrows of Devil's Gate. From the turnoff to Saline Valley, at about 7,200 feet elevation, the road is barely two lanes of asphalt. It winds through desert hills and descends into Little Cowhorn Valley, and then crosses Joshua Flats. After vast, low-lying Eureka Valley appears, you'll begin an ear-popping descent while looking out at the Last Chance Range. When you reach South Eureka Valley Road, turn south for the 10-mile (one-way) drive to Eureka Dunes. Archaeologists have found evidence that native people gathered there for thousands of years. Back on the main road, continue through scenic Hanging Rock Canyon, and eventually you will pass an old sulfur mine as you cross the Last Chance Range. You will know you've reached Crankshaft Junction when you see all the old car parts beside the road. From there, the road makes a 4,000-foot plunge to the floor of Death Valley. You will reach pavement about 21 miles from Crankshaft Junction.

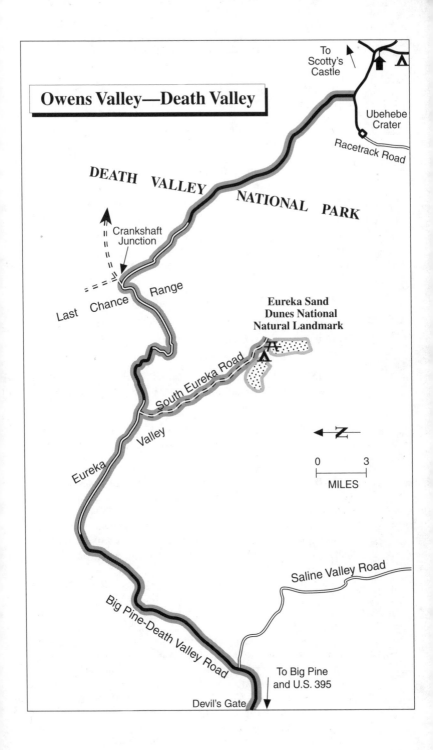

Owens Valley—Death Valley

To Scotty's Castle

Ubehebe Crater

Racetrack Road

DEATH VALLEY NATIONAL PARK

Crankshaft Junction

Last Chance Range

Eureka Sand Dunes National Natural Landmark

South Eureka Road

Eureka Valley

N

0   3
MILES

Saline Valley Road

Big Pine-Death Valley Road

To Big Pine and U.S. 395

Devil's Gate

33

Alabama Hills

LOCATION: At the base of the Sierra Nevada, west of Lone Pine. Inyo County.

HIGHLIGHTS: The Alabama Hills is a jumbled expanse of huge, rounded, honey-brown granite boulders with one of the region's most spectacular backdrops: the peaks of the Muir Crest, which culminate at 14,495-foot Mt. Whitney, the highest point in the contiguous states. The Alabama Hills have been a favorite stage for movie makers and advertisers since the 1920s. They also are a favorite venue for photography and rock climbing. Wildflowers add to this convenient drive during the first two weeks or so of May.

DIFFICULTY: Easy, on graded roads. Spurs are rougher.

TIME & DISTANCE: An hour; 13 miles.

MAPS: Inyo National Forest. ACSC's *Guide to the Eastern Sierra*.

INFORMATION: BLM's Bishop Field Office. Eastern Sierra InterAgency Visitor Center, south of Lone Pine at U.S. 395 and Hwy. 136.

GETTING THERE: From U.S. 395 at Lone Pine, take Whitney Portal Road west, directly toward the mountains, for 2.7 miles. Turn right (north) onto Movie Road.

REST STOPS: Fuel, food and lodging are available in Lone Pine. There are a number of campgrounds in the area. Dispersed camping in the Alabama Hills is discouraged.

THE DRIVE: The 30,000-acre, BLM-managed Alabama Hills Recreation Area is a landscape of dramatic contrasts. Soaring to the west are the peaks of the eastern Sierra, sculpted by glaciers and the effects of water freezing and thawing in the granite's cracks and crevices. The Alabama Hills, however, consist of massive jointed and faulted boulders. They are almost identical in age and composition to the Sierra, but are thought to have been shaped by chemical weathering when the climate was wetter and the rocks were buried. In 1862, a precursor of the fictional Western shootouts filmed here occurred when settlers attacked a Paiute Indian camp, killing 11. When Confederacy sympathizers found gold here, they named their claims the Alabama District, after the Confederate Navy cruiser *Alabama*, which sank 64 Union merchant ships during the Civil War. Union sympathizers countered by naming their mining district, a town, a mountain and a pass after the Union's *Kearsarge*, which sank the *Alabama* in June 1864 off the port of Cherbourg, France. Beginning in the 1920s, Hollywood has made the Alabama Hills familiar to moviegoers as the setting for numerous Westerns and other films. Thus, the road initially crosses an area depicted in so many films that it's dubbed Movie Flat.

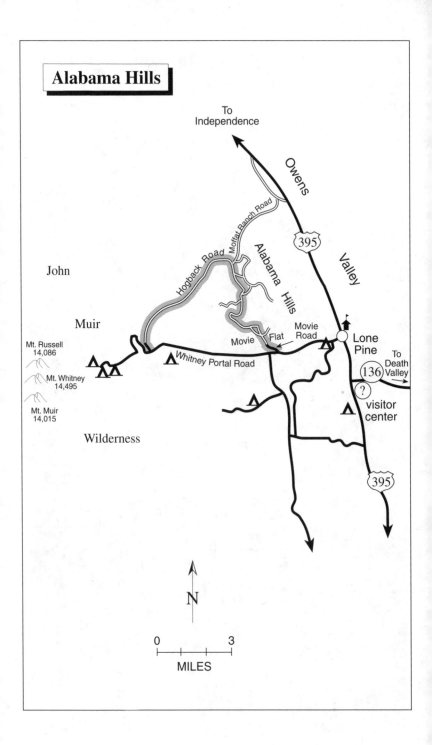

Alabama Hills

To
Independence

Owens

395

Valley

John

Muir

Hogback Road

Moffat Ranch Road

Alabama Hills

Mt. Russell
14,086

Mt. Whitney
14,495

Mt. Muir
14,015

Wilderness

Movie
Flat

Movie
Road

Whitney Portal Road

Lone
Pine

To
Death
136 Valley

? visitor
center

395

N

0   3
MILES

Gunga Din movie site, Alabama Hills *(Tour 7)*

Alabama Hills *(Tour 7)*

Inyo Mountains

LOCATION: East of the Sierra Nevada. Inyo County.

HIGHLIGHTS: With the geologically linked White Mountains (Tour 3), the Inyos form the eastern wall of 10,000-foot-deep Owens Valley. Not as high as the Sierra, they still provide an exhilarating driving experience. In addition to views of the Inyos' canyons and ridges, you will have vistas across Owens Valley to the Sierra, especially from Mazourka Peak and Papoose Flat. You will exit at Death Valley Road (a.k.a. Saline Valley/Eureka Valley Road, Tour 10). This route also connects to The Narrows-Papoose Flat (Tour 5) at Papoose Flat.

DIFFICULTY: Easy to moderate, with short sidehill segments and a rough downhill section to Papoose Flat.

TIME & DISTANCE: 7-8 hours; about 64 miles from Independence to Big Pine, including the side routes I mention.

MAP: Inyo National Forest.

INFORMATION: Inyo National Forest's Mt. Whitney Ranger Station. The Eastern Sierra InterAgency Visitor Center at U.S. 395 and Hwy. 136, south of Lone Pine.

GETTING THERE: Just south of Independence, go east from U.S. 395 on Mazourka Canyon Road (13S05).

REST STOPS: There are good primitive campsites at Badger Flat and elsewhere. No water or facilities are available.

THE DRIVE: When you reach the mountains, veer left (north), following dirt Mazourka Canyon Road (13S05) up the canyon, which runs north-south instead of the usual east-west. At mile 12.3 is the left (west) turn for road 13S05A to Santa Rita Flat, which has a great vista. About 18.1 miles from U.S. 395 is Badger Flat; keep left. In another mile is a right fork that you will follow later. Keeping left, follow a small road (11S01) up to an awesome view from 9,412-foot Mazourka Peak. Return to that right fork you saw earlier and angle northeast past a corral. About 0.1 mile beyond the ruins of Blue Bell Mine, go left. Climb a steep section toward a saddle. Just after going down a dip, you will see a small Y. Descend on the left track. Cross two sidehills, then descend to a small valley. Note the track to the northwest (left) from the valley floor; that's your route (9S15). In 2.3 miles the road may seem to vanish, but it's to the left. Descend a rough section to Papoose Flat, an important food-gathering place for Native Americans for thousands of years. Follow 9S15 north across Papoose Flat. Keep right at the Y just beyond the junction with road 10S07, and descend via switchbacks to Death Valley/Saline Valley/Eureka Valley Road. Big Pine is about 13 miles to the left (west), via that road and Hwy. 168.

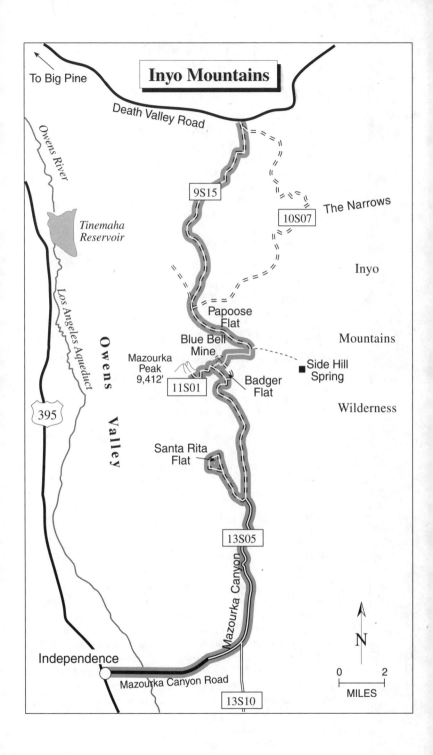

Inyo Mountains

Cerro Gordo

LOCATION: Southern Inyo Mountains. Inyo County.

HIGHLIGHTS: Climbing 4,400 feet to the semi-occupied ghost town of Cerro Gordo provides stunning views across Owens Valley to the High Sierra. Cerro Gordo (Spanish for "Fat Hill") is the name of the nearby 9,184-foot peak, the 19th century town and the mines that produced silver, lead and zinc. Silver was discovered here in 1865. By 1871, the town had nearly 2,000 people. The silver boom ended by 1879, but in the early 1900s Cerro Gordo became the nation's foremost producer of high-grade zinc. The mines produced intermittently until 1936. The descent from the Inyos to Death Valley National Park, where you will link up with Saline Valley Road (Tour 10), offers terrific views as well.

DIFFICULTY: Easy, but the final stretch to the town is a narrow shelf road. The descent to Death Valley National Park is rocky, and the road is subject to washouts.

TIME & DISTANCE: 2.5 hours; 33 miles.

MAP: ACSC's *Guide to Death Valley National Park*.

INFORMATION: Inyo National Forest's Mt. Whitney Ranger Station. The Eastern Sierra InterAgency Visitor Center at Hwys. 395 and 136 south of Lone Pine. Cerro Gordo.

GETTING THERE: It seems logical to start from U.S. 395 south of Lone Pine, taking Hwy. 136 southeast to Keeler, then turning northeast onto Cerro Gordo Road. So that's how I describe it. However, going in the opposite direction so that you can view the Sierra more easily is arguably the better way.

REST STOPS: Lone Pine has all services. Lodging is available at Cerro Gordo; call ahead.

THE DRIVE: Prepare for some of the most beautiful 7.7 miles you'll ever drive. The road immediately begins ascending the Inyos, and by mile 2.7 is threading through a narrow canyon of sheer, colorful rock walls. You will soon see remains of Cerro Gordo's heyday: tunnels, trams and other relics. At mile 4.6 a knoll with a breathtaking view of the Sierra Nevada is on the left. From here, the road dips, bends and winds its way through the mountains, colored by wildflowers if it's spring. At about mile 5.4 you'll pass Joshua trees, and soon the road becomes a narrow shelf. Mile 7.7 will find you at privately owned Cerro Gordo, where the American Hotel (1871) presides over town. Continue to the crest, descend to San Lucas Canyon on a rocky road, then turn right (southeast) at a T at about mile 12.9. You'll soon be driving along the western boundary of Death Valley National Park. At mile 17.5 keep left. Cross Lee Flat, and pass through a Joshua-tree forest. At mile 24.5 is Saline Valley Road. Hwy. 190 is 8.2 miles to the right.

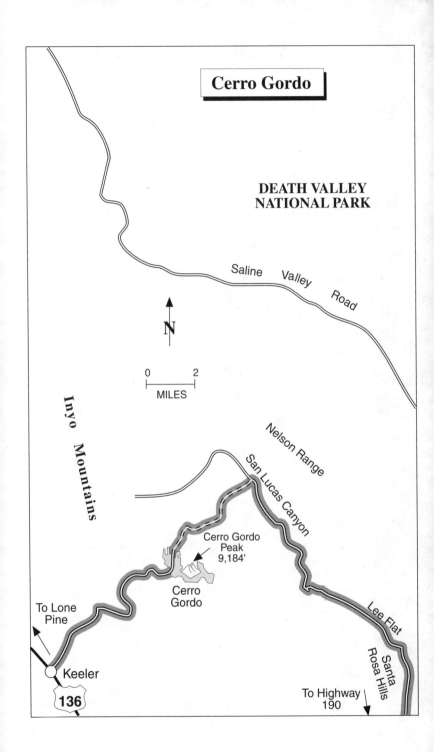

Cerro Gordo

DEATH VALLEY
NATIONAL PARK

Saline Valley Road

N

0   2
MILES

Nelson Range

Inyo Mountains

San Lucas Canyon

Cerro Gordo
Peak
9,184'

Cerro
Gordo

Lee Flat

To Lone
Pine

Keeler

136

Santa Rosa Hills

To Highway
190

Saline Valley Road

LOCATION: East of the Inyo Mountains, on the northwestern edge of Death Valley National Park. Inyo County.

HIGHLIGHTS: Saline Valley Road traverses a basin-and-range landscape of epic scale, with towering mountains flanking a remote valley complete with clothing-optional hot springs, a verdant salt marsh, sand dunes and historic mine sites. It's a busy place in spring, but very hot in summer.

DIFFICULTY: Easy, but changeable. You may encounter severe washboarding on this remote 2WD, high-clearance road. North and South passes can be closed in winter and spring. Floods can close the road in summer.

TIME & DISTANCE: 5-6 hours; about 100 miles starting at Big Pine, on U.S. 395, and ending at Hwy. 190.

MAPS: ACSC's *Guide to Death Valley National Park.* Trails Illustrated's *Death Valley National Park* topo map (No. 221).

INFORMATION: Death Valley National Park. Eastern Sierra InterAgency Visitor Center at Lone Pine.

GETTING THERE: From U.S. 395 at Big Pine, take Hwy. 168 east for 2.2 miles, then take a right onto the Big Pine-Death Valley Road, a.k.a. Saline Valley-Eureka Valley Road. About 13.1 miles later Waucoba-Saline Valley Road branches off to the southeast.

REST STOPS: Soak and camp (primitive) at Lower Warm Spring and Palm Spring.

THE DRIVE: Inhospitable as Saline Valley appears, its marsh supports plant and animal life, and archaeologists have found evidence of human habitation going back at least 10,000 years. Drive through the scenic narrows of Devil's Gate on the road to Death Valley (Tour 6). Where Saline Valley Road turns southeast, you're at about 7,500 feet above sea level. Saline Valley, in contrast, is at about 1,100 feet. After 14.5 miles you will see a pale, forbidding trough in the distance. That's Saline Valley, flanked by the Inyo Mountains and the Last Chance Range. The road forms the park's western boundary in these parts. You will drop fast now, crossing washes that suggest the power of flash floods. Almost 33 miles from Big Pine-Death Valley Road you will see a painted rock on the left, at the entrance to the side road to a series of popular hot springs. Beyond that is a salt marsh, an odd sight here. The ruins of salt works and a tram, built between 1911-1913 to transport salt over the Inyo Mountains, can be seen about 2 miles south of it. The road will pass the rough and risky 4x4 trail to Lippincott Mine and enter Grapevine Canyon, with its wild grapevines, willows and Joshua trees. At the top of the canyon is South Pass, where you can turn off to Hidden Valley (Tour 11) or descend to Hwy. 190.

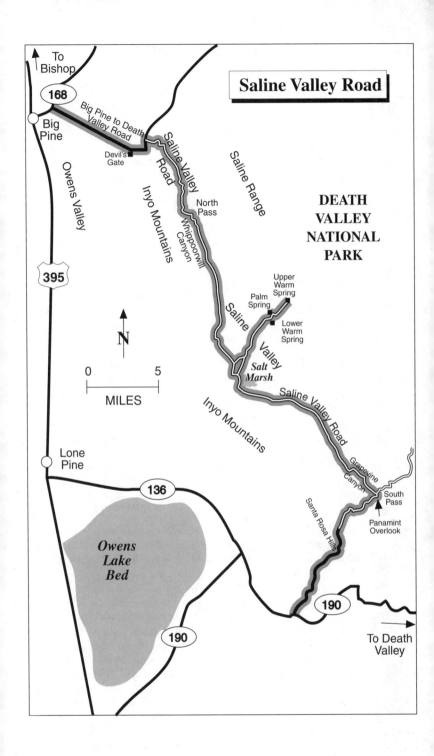

Saline Valley Road

To Bishop

168

Big Pine

Big Pine to Death Valley Road

Owens Valley

Devil's Gate

Saline Valley Road

Inyo Mountains

Whippoorwill Canyon

North Pass

Saline Range

DEATH VALLEY NATIONAL PARK

Upper Warm Spring

Palm Spring

Lower Warm Spring

Saline

395

Valley

N

0   5

MILES

Salt Marsh

Saline Valley Road

Inyo Mountains

Lone Pine

136

Grapevine Canyon

South Pass

Panamint Overlook

Owens Lake Bed

Santa Rosa Hills

190

190

To Death Valley

Hidden Valley

LOCATION: Death Valley National Park. Inyo County.

HIGHLIGHTS: This high (about 5,000 feet) and remote valley has a large Joshua tree forest, old mines, springtime wildflowers and worthwhile side routes. It is cooler than lower Saline, Eureka and Death valleys, and gets more precipitation. The limestone narrows of Lost Burro Gap are scenic, and the remains of Lost Burro Mine recall the valley's bygone bustle. This drive connects to Racetrack Valley Road (Tour 12) at the north end and Saline Valley Road (Tour 10) at the south end.

DIFFICULTY: Easy, but changeable. The Hunter Mountain segment will probably be closed in winter and spring by ice and snow. Check ahead.

TIME & DISTANCE: This is a full day. It's 19.7 miles from Ubehebe Crater to Teakettle Junction via Racetrack Valley Road. It's almost 25 miles from Teakettle Junction over Hunter Mountain to Saline Valley Road at South Pass. It's 15.6 miles from South Pass to Hwy. 190 via Saline Valley Road. The side roads add many more miles.

MAPS: ACSC's *Guide to Death Valley National Park*. Trails Illustrated's *Death Valley National Park* topo map (No. 221).

INFORMATION: Death Valley National Park.

GETTING THERE: Turn south from Racetrack Valley Road at Teakettle Junction, or northeast off Saline Valley Road at South Pass. If you go in spring and the Hunter Mountain segment is closed, enter Hidden Valley from Teakettle Junction and then backtrack when you're done.

REST STOPS: Historic Lost Burro Mine is worth a visit.

THE DRIVE: At Teakettle Junction, drive up the gravel wash into narrow Lost Burro Gap. Beyond the gap, a 4WD road climbs northeast high into the Cottonwood Mountains to White Top Mountain, adding about 20 scenic miles round-trip. At the same junction is the turnoff to the old Lost Burro Mine (1 mile), a historic site worth seeing. The graded road ahead winds through Hidden Valley to Ulida Flat, a Joshua-tree forest and an old mining area. Beyond that, it narrows for the rougher climb up Hunter Mountain. When the climbing ends and the better road begins, watch for a side road that goes north. It ends in about 5 miles at a point overlooking Hidden Valley and Racetrack Valley. It starts out as a high-clearance 2WD road, then becomes a 4WD road for the last mile or so. On the main road, continue over Hunter Mountain to Saline Valley Road at South Pass. If you're driving over Hunter Mountain from Saline Valley Road at South Pass, in about 7.2 miles—just before the road becomes rough and narrow and descends to Hidden Valley—go left (north) on the side road mentioned above before continuing down to Hidden Valley.

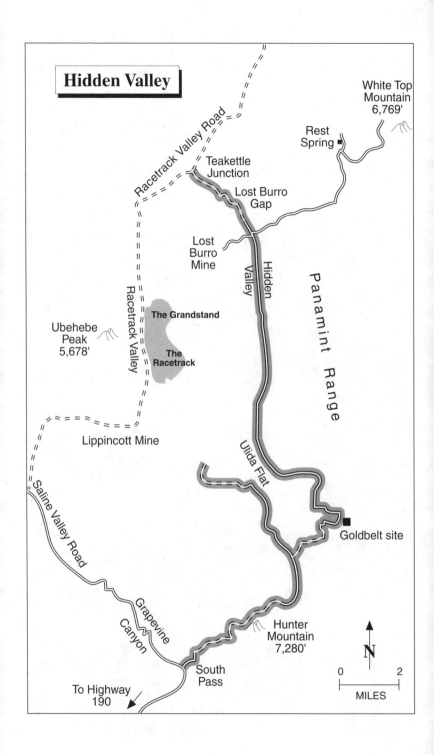

Hidden Valley

White Top Mountain 6,769'

Rest Spring

Teakettle Junction

Lost Burro Gap

Racetrack Valley Road

Lost Burro Mine

Hidden Valley

Panamint Range

The Grandstand

Ubehebe Peak 5,678'

Racetrack Valley

The Racetrack

Lippincott Mine

Ulida Flat

Goldbelt site

Saline Valley Road

Grapevine Canyon

Hunter Mountain 7,280'

N

South Pass

0   2
MILES

To Highway 190

Hidden Valley *(Tour 11)*

Racetrack's "moving rocks" *(Tour 12)*

Racetrack Valley Road

LOCATION: Death Valley National Park. Inyo County.

HIGHLIGHTS: Ubehebe Crater; a Joshua tree forest; the ancient dry lakebed (playa) called The Racetrack, and its famous "moving rocks." This road connects with the Hidden Valley tour (No. 11). Experienced four-wheelers may want to try the unmaintained, rock-strewn, narrow and badly eroded 6.9-mile Lippincott Road from the south end of The Racetrack down to Saline Valley Road (Tour 10).

DIFFICULTY: Racetrack Valley Road is usually easy, but conditions can deteriorate. It's often badly washboarded. Do not drive on The Racetrack playa, and don't walk on it if it's muddy. Risky Lippincott Road, an unmaintained 4x4 trail at the south end of Racetrack Valley Road, is usually in poor condition. It's typically eroded, narrow and washed out in places. I drove it without incident, but I will rate it potentially difficult because it's unpredictable.

TIME & DISTANCE: All day; about 63 miles round-trip from Ubehebe Crater to Lippincott Mine.

MAPS: ACSC's *Guide to Death Valley National Park*. Trails Illustrated's *Death Valley National Park* topo map (No. 221).

INFORMATION: Death Valley National Park.

GETTING THERE: It begins at Ubehebe Crater, northwest of the Grapevine Ranger Station.

REST STOPS: There's a portable toilet at Lippincott Mine, 1.6 miles beyond The Racetrack. Camping is not permitted along Racetrack Valley Road, but there are primitive campsites at Lippincott Mine, a solitary place to camp indeed.

THE DRIVE: Before setting out, gaze into Ubehebe Crater, an explosion pit a half-mile wide and 750 feet deep, caused when water came into contact with molten rock that had worked its way up through fissures. Driving between the Cottonwood Mountains to the south and the Last Chance Range to the north, the road climbs gradually from about 2,400 feet at the start to almost 5,000 feet amid the Joshua-tree forest flanking Tin Pass. There begins the gradual descent past unmistakable Tea Kettle Junction (22 miles from the start) and the turnoff to Hidden Valley, to about 3,700 feet at The Racetrack. Rising from the playa is The Grandstand, the tip of a mountain buried long ago by material eroded from the surrounding mountains. If the surface is dry, walk out to it. There is a parking area and sign with information about the moving rocks at the south end of The Racetrack. From there, walk upwards of a mile toward the rocky slopes at the southern edge of the playa. One theory is that wind pushes the rocks, which can be quite large and heavy, when precipitation makes the playa slick. If you do find some, do not disturb them so that other visitors can enjoy them as well.

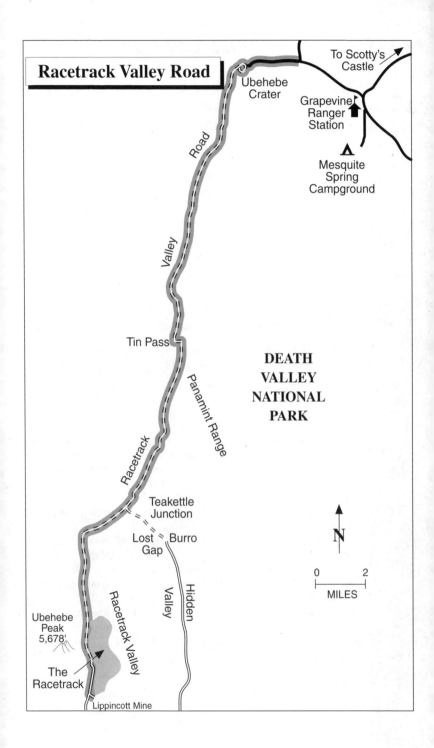

Racetrack Valley Road

To Scotty's Castle

Ubehebe Crater

Grapevine Ranger Station

Mesquite Spring Campground

Road

Valley

Tin Pass

DEATH VALLEY NATIONAL PARK

Panamint Range

Racetrack

Teakettle Junction

Lost Gap

Burro

Valley

Hidden

N

0   2
MILES

Racetrack Valley

Ubehebe Peak 5,678'

The Racetrack

Lippincott Mine

Titus Canyon

LOCATION: Death Valley National Park, in the Grapevine Mountains. Nye County, Nevada, and Inyo County, California.

HIGHLIGHTS: This is one of the park's most beautiful and popular off-highway drives. It includes the ghost town of Leadfield, a narrow, high-walled canyon through the Grapevines' western slope, and petroglyphs and possible desert bighorn sheep at Klare Spring.

DIFFICULTY: Easy. It can only be driven east to west. It's no longer closed in summer, but if you go then it's recommended that you travel with a second vehicle for safety.

TIME & DISTANCE: 2-3 hours; 27 miles.

MAPS: ACSC's *Guide to Death Valley National Park.* Trails Illustrated's *Death Valley National Park* topo map (No. 221).

INFORMATION: Death Valley National Park provides a free informational handout about Titus Canyon.

GETTING THERE: The road begins in Nevada, 2.7 miles northeast of the park boundary and 6.1 miles southwest of Beatty, off Hwy. 374.

REST STOPS: There are a number of places along the way, including Leadfield, where you'll see old mines and buildings. There is no camping along the road.

THE DRIVE: Titus Canyon was named in 1906 for a young mining engineer, Morris Titus, who disappeared in the canyon when searching for water. The Titus Canyon road will take you from the Amargosa Desert up switchbacks to Red Pass, at about 4,200 feet, through the Grapevine Mountains, then down to about 165 feet above sea level at Death Valley. Along the way you will pass through multicolored volcanic stream, lakebed and ocean deposits. Leadfield was a short-lived mining town founded in 1925 by C.C. Julian, the venture's largest investor. Much money was spent on holes that missed the ore. When they found it, bad luck continued when the engine for the mill failed to arrive. After further mishaps, Julian lost his fortune, and other investors blamed him for their losses. Narrow, high-walled Titus Canyon is beyond Leadfield and Klare Spring, where you can see ancient Native American rock art. The drive ends on the western slope of the Grapevine Mountains, 14.9 miles north of Hwy. 190.

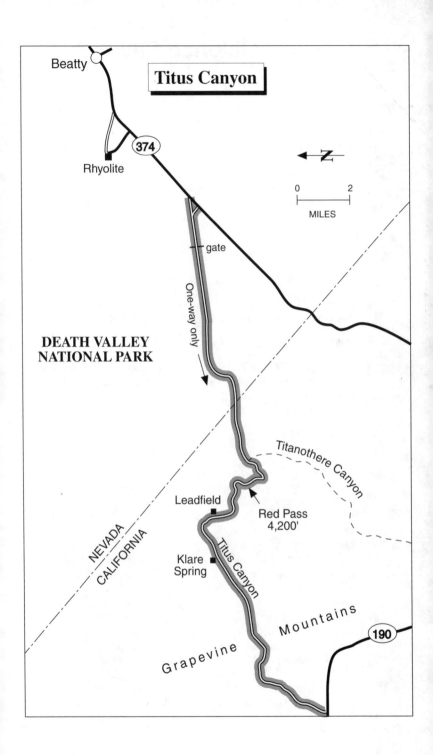

Titus Canyon

Beatty
Rhyolite
374

0 — 2
MILES

N

gate

One-way only

DEATH VALLEY
NATIONAL PARK

Titanothere Canyon

Leadfield

Red Pass
4,200'

Klare
Spring

Titus Canyon

NEVADA
CALIFORNIA

Grapevine

Mountains

190

Chloride City

LOCATION: This loop in eastern Death Valley National Park takes you to the crest of the Funeral Mountains, on the California-Nevada state line. Inyo County.

HIGHLIGHTS: You will have a spectacular bird's-eye view of Death Valley, the Panamint Range and even the Sierra Nevada while visiting the site of Chloride City and Chloride Cliffs. Chloride City was the site of Death Valley's first mining claim (1871). Only a few foundations, shacks, the grave of a fellow known only as James McKay, rusted auto bodies, and other debris remain. It is illegal to collect or remove anything.

DIFFICULTY: Easy to moderate.

TIME & DISTANCE: 2.5 hours; about 20 miles.

MAPS: ACSC's *Guide to Death Valley National Park*. Trails Illustrated's *Death Valley National Park* topo map (No. 221).

INFORMATION: Death Valley National Park.

GETTING THERE: Take Daylight Pass Road/Nevada Hwy. 374 to the park's eastern boundary. Just east of the boundary, on the southeastern side of the highway 8.8 miles southwest of Beatty, Nev., is a dirt road going south. Take it.

REST STOPS: Chloride City and Chloride Cliff. The park does not allow camping for the last 2 miles of the route.

THE DRIVE: You'll start at an elevation of about 3,400 feet and climb to Chloride Cliff, at about 5,400 feet. The road is easy but sections can wash out in heavy rains. Vegetation for the first 11 miles is predominantly creosote bush, but you'll also see sage, box thorn and desert trumpet. The rocks early in the drive are mostly ash deposits from volcanic centers to the east. Rock types change around mile 9.8 to ocean deposits of sand and mud. These deposits are estimated to be 800 million years old. At mile 11 go left and continue on to Chloride City. You will reach a view of Chloride City at mile 12.2. The structures were built after 1903 when this entire region experienced a silver and lead mining boom. Chloride Cliff is another mile ahead beyond the saddle on the other side of the town site. To reach the saddle keep left at the forks. Go left again when you get to the saddle. Follow the road from here to the obvious high point. Walk the last 50 feet to the top of Chloride Cliff. To complete the loop and return to the highway, return to the junction you passed through earlier, back at mile 11, and go left (west) on the 4WD road (moderately difficult) that exits on Daylight Pass Road at Boundary Canyon, about midway between Hell's Gate and Daylight Pass.

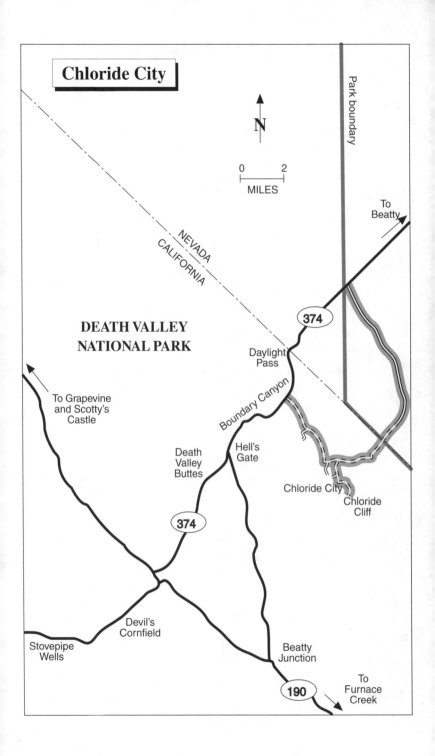

Chloride City

N

0 2
MILES

To Beatty

NEVADA
CALIFORNIA

DEATH VALLEY
NATIONAL PARK

Park boundary

374

Daylight Pass

Boundary Canyon

To Grapevine
and Scotty's
Castle

Death
Valley
Buttes

Hell's
Gate

Chloride City

Chloride
Cliff

374

Devil's
Cornfield

Stovepipe
Wells

Beatty
Junction

To
Furnace
Creek

190

Cottonwood / Marble Canyons

LOCATION: Death Valley National Park, in the Cottonwood Mountains west of Stovepipe Wells. Inyo County.

HIGHLIGHTS: You will follow sandy and rocky desert washes that snake between sheer, narrow limestone walls as the road climbs from sea level to about 3,500 feet. The Cottonwood Canyon road brings you to a flowing spring-fed stream, and ends at a lovely grove. Rougher Marble Canyon is noted for its dramatic narrows and Native American rock art.

DIFFICULTY: Moderate to difficult with sand, gravel, rock and washouts. Marble Canyon is very rocky. The final leg up Cottonwood Canyon may be washed out. Near the end the route is in a narrow stream. You might want to hike that part.

TIME & DISTANCE: 5-6 hours. Cottonwood Canyon is 38 miles round-trip. Marble Canyon adds 5.4 miles round-trip.

MAPS: ACSC's *Guide to Death Valley National Park*. Trails Illustrated's *Death Valley National Park* topo map (No. 221).

INFORMATION: Death Valley National Park.

GETTING THERE: The road begins off Hwy. 190 about 100 feet west of the store in Stovepipe Wells. This also is the campground entrance. Mileages are from the highway.

REST STOPS: The cottonwood grove at the end of the Cottonwood Canyon road is a great place for lunch. Camping is not allowed for the first 8 miles of the Cottonwood Canyon road, or within a quarter-mile of a water source. Stovepipe Wells has a campground, store, fuel, motel and restaurant.

THE DRIVE: Drive about 100 feet from the highway and turn left on the road marked "airstrip." The road is paved for the next half-mile. Keep right at the fork where the pavement ends. The road crosses the valley and climbs onto a bench where desert pavement can be seen. There's a good vista point just before you enter rocky Cottonwood Wash, which leads to the first high-walled narrows. Unusual "balls" of black chert, rock made of microscopic marine organisms called radio-larians, can be seen in the gray limestone outcrop at mile 9.6. These rocks were formed about 400 million years ago in an ancient sea. As you enter the canyon, scan the walls carefully for petroglyphs. Recent figures, made by vandals, are white. The authentic ones, dull gray and weathered, may be 6,000 years old. At mile 11, about a mile beyond the first narrows, the road into high-walled Marble Canyon goes right. It ends in 2.7 miles, at a narrow gap. It's worth continuing on foot, how-ever, to see its spectacular walls and, if you look carefully, its fine (and in some cases vandalized) petroglyphs. Cottonwood Canyon Road (keep left at the entrance to Marble Canyon) continues through an open area, then more narrows. It ends at about mile 19, or when it's too rough to proceed.

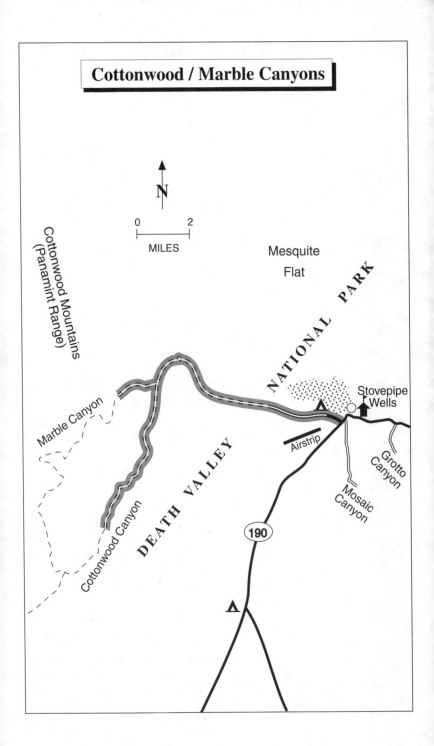

Cottonwood / Marble Canyons

N

0   2

MILES

Cottonwood Mountains
(Panamint Range)

Mesquite

Flat

NATIONAL PARK

Marble Canyon

Stovepipe
Wells

Airstrip

Grotto
Canyon

Cottonwood Canyon

Mosaic
Canyon

DEATH VALLEY

190

Darwin to Darwin Falls

LOCATION: Between Darwin, just outside Death Valley National Park's southwestern boundary, and Hwy. 190 just west of Panamint Springs, inside the park. Inyo County.

HIGHLIGHTS: This is an outstanding alternative to entering the park from the west via Hwy. 190. From the old mining town of Darwin (occupied but not tourist-oriented), it makes long climbs and long, meandering descents through the Darwin Hills, passes between colorful canyon walls and continues to a cottonwood-shaded spring. It provides truly breathtaking vistas across basin-and-range country as it descends to Darwin Falls, a rare year-round 30-foot-high desert waterfall and lush riparian area, and Hwy. 190. It ends a mile west of Panamint Springs.

DIFFICULTY: Easy. Shelf sections may be disconcerting.

TIME & DISTANCE: 1 hour driving time; 15 miles. The hike to Darwin Falls is about 2 miles round-trip (carry water).

MAPS: ACSC's *Guide to Death Valley National Park*. Trails Illustrated's *Death Valley National Park* topo map (No. 221).

INFORMATION: Death Valley National Park. Eastern Sierra InterAgency Visitor Center at Lone Pine.

GETTING THERE: From Hwy. 190 west of the park boundary, turn southeast onto paved Darwin Road (Olancha-Darwin Road on some maps). Follow it to Darwin. There, turn left at the old post office. Set your odometer to 0.

REST STOPS: Stop at China Garden Spring, an old mine site where tall cottonwood trees shade a pond complete with goldfish. Swimming is not allowed at Darwin Falls. Panamint Springs Resort has a motel, campground, restaurant and, by the time you read this, possibly fuel. Darwin has no services.

THE DRIVE: Darwin is named for Darwin French, who explored the area in 1860. Lead and silver were found in the hills here in 1875. The town subsequently became the center of the New Coso Mining District, where gold, zinc and copper also were mined. From Darwin, the road climbs and climbs. Then it makes a long descent, changing from rudimentary asphalt to oiled dirt and then just dirt as it heads into Darwin Canyon. There, if you look closely at the rock walls, you will see strata of severely bent and curved rock. At mile 6.2 the road branches right to make a long climb from the canyon bottom into the hills. You will return to this turnoff. For now, continue along the canyon bottom. About a mile farther is China Garden Spring. From the turnoff at mile 6.2, the road climbs to a crest, then descends into the park and Darwin Canyon again, providing terrific views of mountains and valleys to the north. The turnoff to the Darwin Falls trailhead is 2.8 miles from the crest. Hwy. 190 is 2.4 miles from there.

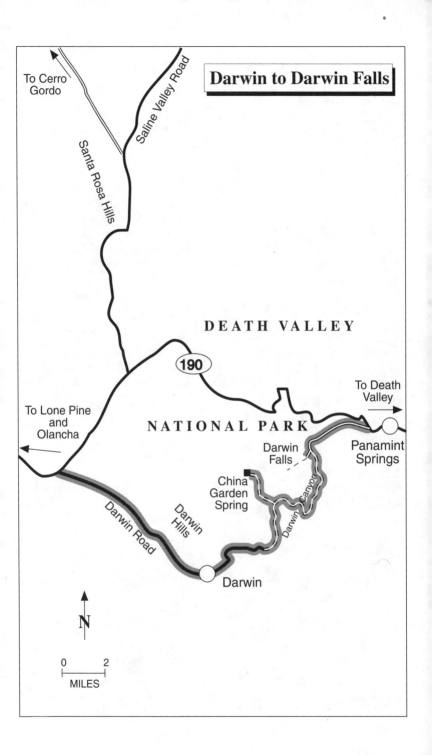

Darwin to Darwin Falls

To Cerro Gordo

Saline Valley Road

Santa Rosa Hills

DEATH VALLEY

190

To Death Valley

To Lone Pine and Olancha

NATIONAL PARK

Darwin Falls

China Garden Spring

Panamint Springs

Darwin Canyon

Darwin Road

Darwin Hills

Darwin

N

0   2
MILES

57

Marble Canyon *(Tour 15)*

Echo Canyon *(Tour 17)*

Echo Canyon

LOCATION: Death Valley National Park, east of Furnace Creek in the Funeral Mountains. Inyo County.

HIGHLIGHTS: Narrow and serpentine Echo Canyon, where gold was discovered in 1905, is conveniently located for travelers who want to sample backroading in Death Valley without a big commitment. It is famous for its sheer, high rock walls, eroded at one point into a hole dubbed Eye of the Needle. At the end of the tour is historic Inyo Mine.

DIFFICULTY: Easy.

TIME & DISTANCE: 3 hours; 19 miles round-trip.

MAPS: ACSC's *Guide to Death Valley National Park*. Trails Illustrated's *Death Valley National Park* topo map (No. 221).

INFORMATION: The park visitor center at Furnace Creek.

GETTING THERE: From Furnace Creek, take Hwy. 190 southeast. About 2.1 miles past the junction with Badwater Road, turn left (east) at the sign for Echo Canyon.

REST STOPS: Inyo Mine is interesting, but like all old mines, it poses hazards. No camping is allowed for the first 2 miles. Food, fuel, camping and lodging are available at Furnace Creek.

THE DRIVE: You will start out at about 400 feet above sea level, and climb to about 3,500 feet. For the first 3 miles the road crosses an alluvial fan. Ahead are the pocked, chocolate-colored mountains and canyon walls of 500 million-year-old limestone and mud sediments from the Cambrian geologic period. Shelled fossils appear in the old seabed and ocean deposits from this period. As you drive, you'll witness the results of the simultaneous geologic actions of uplifting, folding and erosion. At mile 4.7, look up and to your right to see the eroded window, Eye of the Needle. By mile 5.2 you will enter a bowl where you can see even more dramatic geology. At mile 7.7 keep right at the fork. At about mile 8.6 is a junction with a serious 4WD route into Amargosa Valley, Nevada. Finally, at mile 9.6, you will come to Inyo Mine, one of Death Valley's most historic sites. Inadequate financing and lack of water for milling doomed attempts to fully exploit the gold reserves here. It was last worked in 1940. Remember, it's illegal to remove objects from the park.

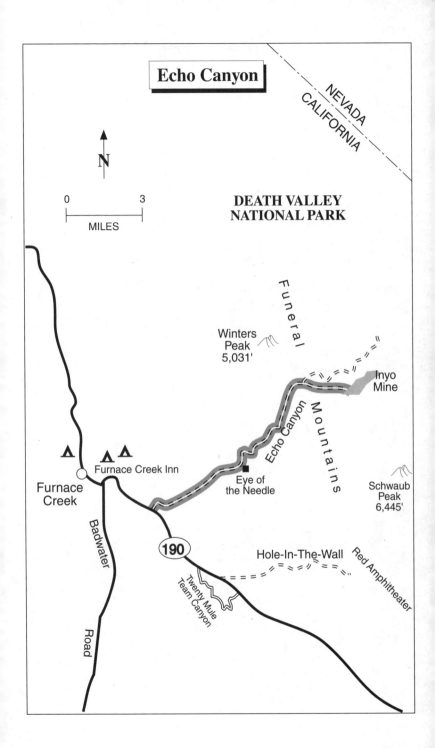

Echo Canyon

NEVADA
CALIFORNIA

N

0   3
MILES

**DEATH VALLEY
NATIONAL PARK**

Funeral

Winters
Peak
5,031'

Inyo
Mine

Echo Canyon

Mountains

Furnace Creek Inn

Eye of
the Needle

Schwaub
Peak
6,445'

Furnace
Creek

Badwater

190

Hole-In-The-Wall

Red Amphitheater

Twenty Mule
Team Canyon

Road

Hole-In-The-Wall

LOCATION: Death Valley National Park, southeast of Furnace Creek in the Funeral Mountains. Inyo County.

HIGHLIGHTS: The 400-foot-high gap called Hole-In-The-Wall and, if you hike beyond road's end, views of Schwaub Peak's striped slopes.

DIFFICULTY: Easy to moderate.

TIME & DISTANCE: An hour if you take only the nearly 8-mile round-trip drive to Hole-In-The-Wall; 2-3 hours if you take the full 12-mile round-trip drive.

MAPS: ACSC's *Guide to Death Valley National Park*. Trails Illustrated's *Death Valley National Park* topo map (No. 221).

INFORMATION: The park visitor center at Furnace Creek.

GETTING THERE: From the Furnace Creek Visitor Center, take Hwy. 190 southeast for 6.8 miles. The route begins in a wash near the 1,000-foot elevation marker along the highway, about midway between the entrance and the exit for Twenty-Mule Team Canyon. Set your odometer at 0.

REST STOPS: Primitive camping is allowed after the first 2 miles. Furnace Creek has lodging, camping, food and fuel.

THE DRIVE: The road winds through stands of creosote bush and spruce bush for the first 3 miles, and the driving is easy on a solid gravel base. Tan-colored sediments from a lake that existed 6 million years ago become visible at mile 1.2 and continue for the next 2.5 miles. Ripple marks can be seen in some locations. Hole-In-The-Wall is at mile 3.9. It's named for the ridge of sediments that were pushed into a vertical position by the Furnace Creek fault, which is no longer active. The complete ridge, or "wall," can be seen better from the east side. From here, the wall is marked by countless small holes. The roadbed gravel becomes looser and deeper for the next mile, and you will see a unique array of cacti, primarily beavertail, cottontop barrel and cholla. The road ends at mile 6. If you want to hike from there, you will eventually see the spectacular striped slopes of Schwaub Peak in the distance, with Pyramid Peak to the right. Both mountains are made of sediments from a shallow, tropical ocean that covered this area about 400 million years ago. A rock outcrop on the left about 2 miles from the end of the road will give you a close look at these rocks. The orange-hued streaks are chert, a rock made of microscopic marine organisms called radiolarians. The dark rock is limestone. (No collecting or removal of rocks is allowed.)

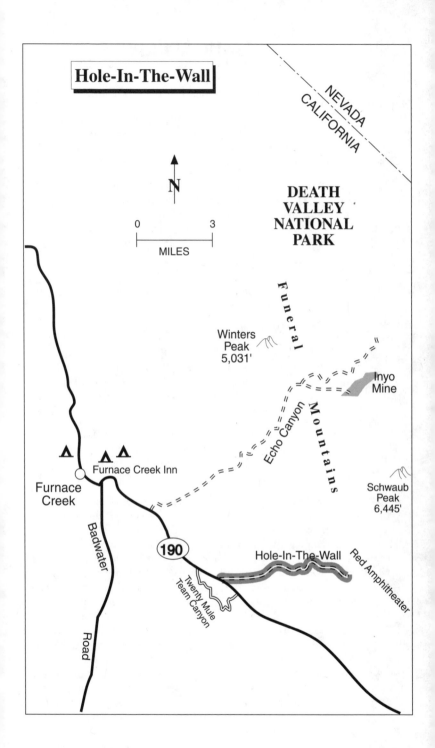

Hole-In-The-Wall

NEVADA
CALIFORNIA

N

0   3
MILES

DEATH
VALLEY
NATIONAL
PARK

Funeral

Winters
Peak
5,031'

Inyo
Mine

Mountains

Echo Canyon

Schwaub
Peak
6,445'

Furnace Creek Inn

Furnace
Creek

Badwater

190

Hole-In-The-Wall

Red Amphitheater

Twenty Mule
Team Canyon

Road

Butte Valley

LOCATION: Death Valley National Park. Inyo County.

HIGHLIGHTS: This tour climbs from about –165 feet in Death Valley to about 4,500 feet in Butte Valley, in the Panamint Range. There are a number of maintained old cabins that you can stay in. You may see wild burros as well.

DIFFICULTY: Easy from Badwater Road to Warm Spring Mine, on a rocky 2WD road. From there it's much rockier, earning a moderate rating. It improves by the time you reach the valley. I rate the segment from Butte Valley over Mengel Pass to the mouth of Goler Wash moderate. The road to Ballarat is 2WD. There is flash flood danger.

TIME & DISTANCE: 4-5 hours; 55 miles.

MAPS: ACSC's *Guide to Death Valley National Park*. Trails Illustrated's *Death Valley National Park* topo map (No. 221).

INFORMATION: Death Valley National Park.

GETTING THERE: Take Badwater Road 42.2 miles south from Hwy. 190, then go west on West Side Road. Or take Hwy. 178 west from Hwy. 127 near Shoshone. About 30 miles from Hwy. 127 (or 3.8 miles after the road bends north and becomes Badwater Road) go west on West Side Road.

REST STOPS: The cabins, maintained by users, are free, and first-come first served. Camping is not allowed for the first 2 miles of Warm Spring Canyon/Butte Valley Road. Primitive camping is OK thereafter, but inquire about regulations.

THE DRIVE: From Badwater Road, cross the wash of the Amargosa River, in a valley that once lay beneath ice-age Lake Manly. At mile 2.9 go left (west) onto Warm Spring Canyon/Butte Valley Road, which climbs through Warm Spring Canyon past billion-year-old ocean sediments. Death Valley got its name when, in the winter of 1849, several pioneer families became lost. After help arrived they made their way here, and one turned and said, "Good-bye, death valley." At mile 14 are some defunct talc mines, including Warm Spring Mine. You'll soon see an old stamp mill, a relic of gold mining farther up the canyon that dates back to the 1870s. By 18.2 you're out of the canyon. Ahead rise the upturned ocean sediments of Striped Butte. West of it is 7,196-ft. Manly Peak. Soon you'll see the so-called Geologist's Cabin, built in the 1930s. Butte Valley Road climbs to Mengel Pass, then drops into Goler Wash, long famous as being very rough but now somewhat improved. Just before Sourdough Spring and the park boundary a road goes left, up a side canyon, to the Barker Ranch, hideout of 1960s cult leader Charles Manson. He was arrested here on Oct. 12, 1969, and was later linked to Los Angeles-area murders. Continue to Panamint Valley, then go north past a gold mine to Ballarat, an 1890s gold mining town. There, go left to Trona-Wildhorse Road.

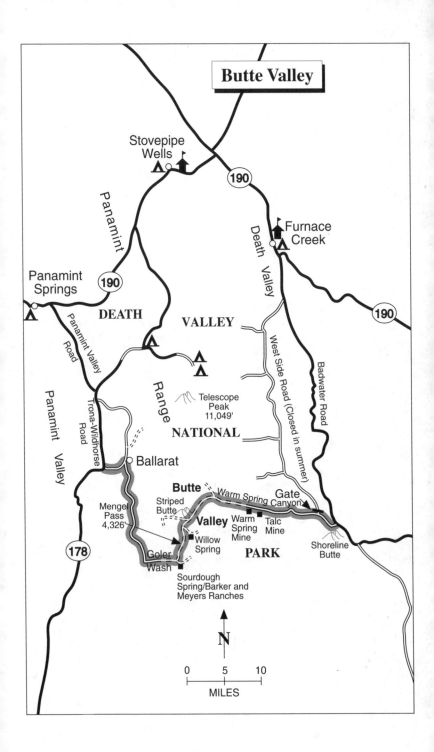

Butte Valley

Trona Pinnacles

LOCATION: In San Bernardino County about 16 miles east of Ridgecrest, a city just east of U.S. 395 near the Kern County/San Bernardino County line.

HIGHLIGHTS: Trona Pinnacles National Natural Landmark encompasses one of the most outstanding collections of tufa towers (calcium carbonate deposits) in the United States. You may even get to watch a sci-fi film being made.

DIFFICULTY: Easy.

TIME & DISTANCE: 1-2 hours; 11 miles.

MAP: ACSC's *San Bernardino County*.

INFORMATION: BLM's Ridgecrest Field Office.

GETTING THERE: From Ridgecrest, take Hwy. 178 (Trona Road) northeast for 16.6 miles. The turnoff to Trona Pinnacles is well-marked. You can see the tufa towers from the highway, rising from the gently sloping expanse of Searles Valley.

REST STOPS: Primitive camping is allowed. Ridgecrest has all services.

THE DRIVE: Here you will wind through more than 500 towers, or pinnacles, some as high as 140 feet. They rise from the bed of Searles Dry Lake. Their size easily eclipses the famous tufa towers at Mono Lake. The pinnacles developed between 10,000 and 100,000 years ago during the Pleistocene Epoch, when ancient Searles Lake formed a link in a chain of interconnected lakes fed by regular rainfall and runoff from the retreating glaciers of the Sierra Nevada. At peak periods the lake reached depths of 640 feet and overflowed into Panamint Valley and Death Valley. Its shoreline is still visible as horizontal banding on the hillsides northwest of the pinnacles. The pinnacles were formed underwater by the interaction of blue-green algae and chemical and geothermal conditions. Hot springs welled up through fault-line fractures to introduce calcium-rich ground water, which combined with carbonates and formed calcium-carbonate deposits. Algae bonded with the deposits, creating the pinnacles. When the lake dried up, the spires remained. You will cross the dried mud at the southern end of the lakebed, following road RM 143. If the lakebed is wet and muddy, don't attempt to cross it. There are great photo opportunities in this odd landscape, which is why photographers and filmmakers often use the setting.

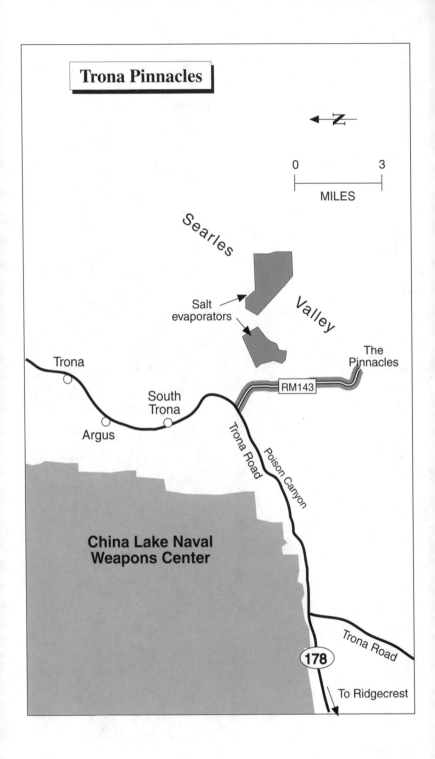

Trona Pinnacles

N

0   3
MILES

Searles Valley

Salt evaporators

The Pinnacles

Trona

South Trona

Argus

RM143

Trona Road

Poison Canyon

China Lake Naval Weapons Center

178   Trona Road

To Ridgecrest

Trona Pinnacles *(Tour 20)*

Afton Canyon *(Tour 26)*

Burro Schmidt's Tunnel

LOCATION: In the El Paso Mountains, just east of Red Rock Canyon State Park. Kern County.

HIGHLIGHTS: In the early 1900s, William H. "Burro" Schmidt, said to have been a tuberculosis victim, arrived in Last Chance Canyon, a mining area that had been occupied by Indians for thousands of years. Beginning in 1906, Schmidt spent 32 years tunneling through the El Pasos, ending up with a 2,087-foot hole that today still connects the interior region of the El Pasos to a panorama of the Fremont Valley. The old cabin there has long been occupied by elderly, friendly and talkative Tonie Seger.

DIFFICULTY: Easy.

TIME & DISTANCE: 2 hours; 16 miles. You can link up with Tour 22, Last Chance Canyon.

MAPS: USGS' *Saltdale NW* and *Garlock* 7.5-minute topo maps. ACSC's *Kern County*. BLM's *Cuddeback Lake* Desert Access Guide.

INFORMATION: BLM's Ridgecrest Field Office.

GETTING THERE: From Hwy. 14 south of Red Rock Canyon State Park, take Red Rock-Randsburg Road northeast for 11 miles. Turn left (north) onto road EP100. You may see a steel drum marked "Burro Schmidt's Tunnel." Set the odometer to 0. Another primary access is to take Hwy. 14 for 10 miles north of Red Rock Canyon State Park's Abbott Drive, then turn right (southeast) onto Hart Road (EP15; also shown as EP155 on some maps) at the billboards. Then follow the signs.

REST STOPS: Red Rock Canyon State Park has a campground and picnic areas. Undeveloped sites can be found on BLM land.

THE DRIVE: Road EP100 heads up Mesquite Canyon to a pass at mile 3.9. From there it drops into broad Last Chance Canyon. At mile 4.9 road EP15, to Schmidt's Tunnel, will be on the left. Go left, and in 2.6 miles you'll be at the 1930s cabin occupied by Tonie Seger. The cabin is part of the U.S. Bureau of Land Management's Adopt-A-Cabin program, through which the BLM and volunteers work to preserve historic structures. Visitors can walk through the tunnel, which is about 200 yards from the cabin. Afterwards, you might continue down EP15 to Pleasant Valley. There, you can continue on the Last Chance Canyon tour or go north a short distance to a junction. There, go east past another Depression-era cabin, Bickel Camp, then return to Red Rock-Randsburg Road via roads EP30 and EP100.

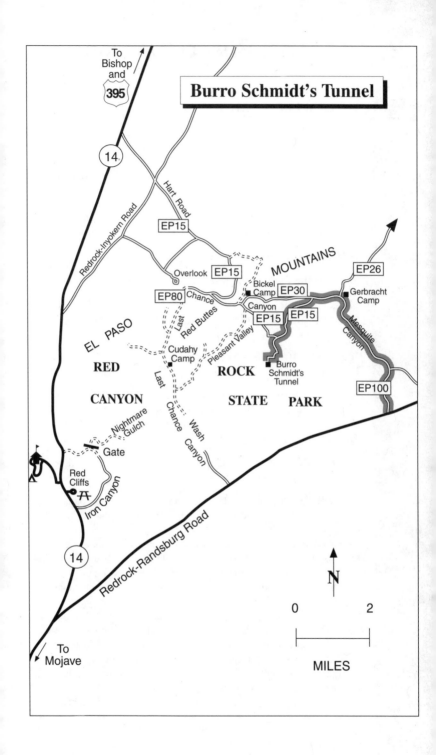

Last Chance Canyon

LOCATION: In the El Paso Mountains of Red Rock Canyon State Park and vicinity. Kern County.

HIGHLIGHTS: Indians occupied the canyon for thousands of years, leaving numerous archaeological sites throughout the area, which is famous as well for colorful cliffs of sedimentary and volcanic rock. In 1893 gold was found in the area, spurring a variety of mining activities. Miscreants, eccentrics, squatters and filmmakers found their way here in the decades to come. Some left behind structures of historic importance. The Bureau of Land Management is developing the Bonanza Trail, a tour route to highlight the sites and the area's history.

DIFFICULTY: Easy to moderate.

TIME & DISTANCE: 2-3 hours; about 20 miles.

MAPS: The park's map. USGS' *Saltdale* NW and *Garlock* 7.5-minute topo maps. ACSC's *Kern County*. BLM's *Cuddeback Lake* Desert Access Guide.

INFORMATION: Red Rock Canyon State Park. BLM's Ridgecrest Field Office.

GETTING THERE: From Hwy. 14 south of the park, take Randsburg-Red Rock Road northeast for 11 miles. Turn left (north) onto road EP100. You may see a steel drum marked "Burro Schmidt's Tunnel." Set your odometer to 0.

REST STOPS: The park has camping and picnic areas. There are primitive campsites in the area as well.

THE DRIVE: Road EP100 heads up Mesquite Canyon to a pass. From there it drops into broad Last Chance Canyon. A mile farther road EP15, to Burro Schmidt's Tunnel (Tour 21), will be on the left. If you keep to the right, on EP30, in another mile is Bickle Camp, a Depression-era mining cabin. Just beyond Bickle Camp is another junction with EP15; go left, down Pleasant Valley, beginning the long loop around Red Buttes. Keep to the right at the next two junctions. At about mile 8.3 you will enter the state park. A couple of miles more and you will cross two washes. At the second one, angle right and follow the wash for 0.4 mile, then follow the road where it climbs out of the wash and continues north into the narrowing canyon. Soon you will see the remains of Cudahy Camp, once a residential area for miners. Just beyond that is a small oasis, which the route bypasses by making a left up a steep and rough 4WD section. It goes around the wetland, passes the dead-end road to Dry Falls, then drops back into the wash and continues up the canyon. 0.2 mile after you emerge from this narrow stretch of canyon, Hart Road (EP15; shown as EP155 on some maps) will be on your left. Take it to Redrock-Inyokern Road or Hwy. 14.

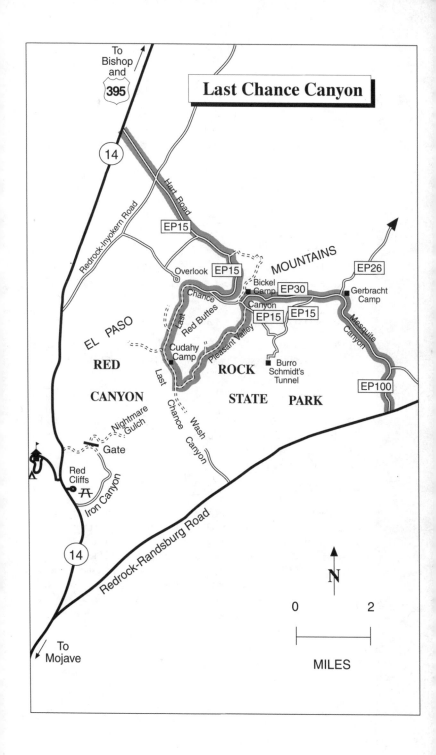

Last Chance Canyon

Iron Canyon

LOCATION: Red Rock Canyon State Park. Kern County.

HIGHLIGHTS: This is a short and convenient loop that begins and ends on Hwy. 14. It offers the chance to experience the park's multi-colored, intricately eroded cliffs of uplifted sedimentary and volcanic rock without a big time commitment. If you're heading north or south on the highway, don't pass it up. If you have more time, it also provides access to Nightmare Gulch, an exceptionally beautiful and narrow canyon where golden eagles and prairie falcons nest. (Nightmare Gulch is closed to all access from Feb. 1 to July 1 to protect raptors during nesting. July through February the 4WD road is closed to vehicles from the 16th of the month through the last day of the month.)

DIFFICULTY: Iron Canyon is an easy, 2WD high-clearance route, although a short uphill segment at the north end may require 4WD. The park lists Nightmare Gulch as a "serious" 4WD route.

TIME & DISTANCE: 30 minutes; 2.9 miles.

MAPS: The park's rudimentary map is adequate. The USGS' *Cantil* and *Saltdale NW* 7.5-minute topo maps are useful, but the latter omits the final leg from Nightmare Gulch to Hwy. 14.

INFORMATION: Red Rock Canyon State Park.

GETTING THERE: Take Hwy. 14 to Red Rock Canyon State Park. The drive starts on the east side of the highway, about 0.4 mile south of Abbott Drive and 0.1 mile north of the highway bridge. Set your odometer to 0 here.

REST STOPS: The park has a campground and picnic areas.

THE DRIVE: From the highway, which passes through the beautiful and ancient travel corridor we call Red Rock Canyon, the road follows a wash through low desert hills. Ahead rise varicolored cliffs of pinks, reds, grays and browns. At mile 1.7 is the gated turnoff to Nightmare Gulch, and just beyond that the road crosses several washes to bring you to the base of Scenic Cliffs, walls of spectacularly colored and ornately eroded sediments capped by harder volcanic rock. By mile 2.4 you are winding up a narrow, serpentine ravine below the cliffs, beyond which is a steep and rougher segment of road. You will arrive at the highway a short distance beyond that.

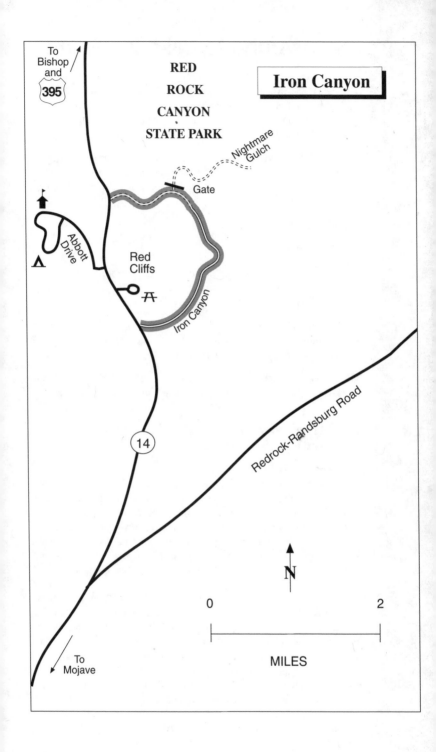

Iron Canyon

RED
ROCK
CANYON
STATE PARK

Nightmare Gulch

Gate

Abbott Drive

Red Cliffs

Iron Canyon

Redrock-Randsburg Road

14

To Bishop and 395

To Mojave

N

0   2

MILES

Jawbone to Lake Isabella

LOCATION: In the Piute Mountains of the southern Sierra Nevada; east of Bakersfield and north of Tehachapi. Between Hwy. 14 south of Red Rock Canyon State Park and Bodfish, near Lake Isabella. Sequoia National Forest. Kern County.

HIGHLIGHTS: You will experience the transition from the Mojave Desert to the forests of the southern Sierra as you climb from 2,500 feet to over 8,000 feet. The descent to Kern Valley and Bodfish via a narrow shelf road is spectacular.

DIFFICULTY: Easy.

TIME & DISTANCE: 3 hours; 53 miles.

MAPS: ACSC's *Kern County*. Sequoia National Forest. At Jawbone Station get a copy of *East Kern County Off-Highway Vehicle Riding Areas & Trails*.

INFORMATION: BLM's Jawbone Station information center, near the junction of Jawbone Canyon Road and Hwy. 14. Sequoia National Forest, Greenhorn Ranger District.

GETTING THERE: From Hwy. 14 about 1.2 miles south of Red Rock-Randsburg Road, take the Jawbone Canyon/Kelso Valley exit. Follow Jawbone Canyon Road west.

REST STOPS: BLM's Jawbone Station. You will find all services at Bodfish and Lake Isabella.

THE DRIVE: Jawbone Canyon Road passes through an off-highway vehicle area, and the pavement ends about 4.1 miles from Hwy. 14, after you pass two large pipelines of the Los Angeles Aqueduct. Ahead is a green-blue hill, Blue Point, which you'll reach at mile 4.7. From there the route climbs into semi-arid foothills, providing outstanding vistas across the Mojave Desert. The hills become dotted first with Joshua trees, then pinyon pines and junipers, then oak woodlands and conifers—changes that signal the transition from one climatic zone to another. The road will eventually descend into pretty Kelso Valley, reaching a junction at about mile 17.8. Here, Kelso Valley Road goes north. Take Jawbone Canyon Road (589) west through the junction, following the sign for Piute Mountain. The road will bend southwest and cross a meadow. Then it turns west and climbs into the Piute Mountains. From there you will ascend the steep and narrow switchbacks of Geringer Grade and enter Sequoia National Forest. Continue north to the junction with Piute Mountain Road (501) and forest road 27S02 (Saddle Spring Road/Piute Mountain Road). At the junction at about mile 31.1, take 27S02 left (west). It will eventually make a thrilling descent to paved Caliente-Bodfish Road (483), just south of Bodfish.

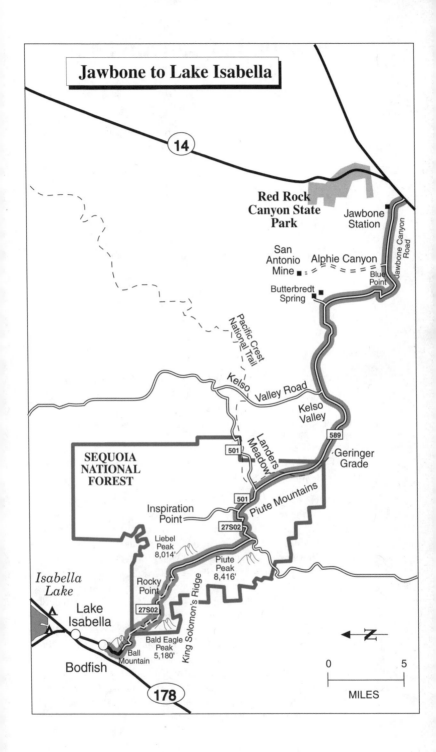

Jawbone to Lake Isabella

Red Rock
Canyon State
Park

Jawbone
Station

San
Antonio   Alphie Canyon
Mine

Blue
Point

Jawbone Canyon Road

Butterbredt
Spring

Pacific Crest National Trail

Kelso   Valley Road

Kelso
Valley

589

Landers Meadow

501

Geringer
Grade

SEQUOIA
NATIONAL
FOREST

501

Inspiration
Point

Piute Mountains

27S02

Liebel
Peak
8,014'

Piute
Peak
8,416'

Isabella
Lake

Rocky
Point

King Solomon's Ridge

Lake
Isabella

27S02

Bald Eagle
Peak
5,180'

Ball
Mountain

Bodfish

178

N

0   5

MILES

77

Inscription Canyon Loop

LOCATION: Circles the Black Mountain Wilderness, about 30 miles northwest of Barstow. San Bernardino County.

HIGHLIGHTS: You'll drive through a rainbow-colored basin on your way to the Black Mountain area, which has one of the largest concentrations of Native American petroglyphs in the Mojave Desert. Though vandalized, Inscription Canyon has a fine array of petroglyphs, as does Black Canyon. Watch for endangered desert tortoises, which venture onto roads.

DIFFICULTY: Easy. There are many roads out here, and numbers on the signposts don't always match those on the BLM maps. A tip: Stay close to the base of the mountains, until you turn into the mountains at Inscription Canyon.

TIME & DISTANCE: 5-6 hours; about 67 miles.

MAPS: ACSC's *San Bernardino County*. BLM's *Cuddeback Lake* Desert Access Guide.

INFORMATION: BLM's Barstow Field Office.

GETTING THERE: From Main Street in Barstow, turn north onto First Street. Drive over the railroad tracks and the Mojave River. Turn left onto Irwin Road. Follow Irwin Road for 5.9 miles. Turn left onto road EF401, toward Rainbow Basin and Owl Canyon Campground. Mileages begin here.

REST STOPS: The fee campground at Owl Canyon, in Rainbow Basin, has water. Barstow has all services.

THE DRIVE: At mile 2.9 is the turnoff for the 4-mile loop through colorful Rainbow Basin, eroded sediments noted for fossils of mastodons, early pronghorns, camels and three-toed horses. Continuing northwest and then west on EF401, about 10.5 miles from Rainbow Basin is a masonry-enclosed well (note your odometer reading here) and a farm. To the north is the Black Mountain Wilderness. 2.8 miles from the well, turn right (north) onto an unsigned road. (If you miss it, 0.7 mile farther turn right onto road EF373. Follow it north for 2.5 miles, then angle right, into Black Canyon.) Follow the unsigned road north for 2.6 miles along the western edge of the wilderness. When you reach a T junction go right, into Black Canyon, where you can view terrific petroglyphs. The road runs along the western and northern base of Black Mountain. About 6 miles from where you entered Black Canyon is a junction; keep right. In 3.1 miles you will arrive at Inscription Canyon. The 200-yard-long arroyo is lined with petroglyphs, thought to have been created by Kawaiisu or Southern Paiute shamans. From there, take the small two-track that climbs south from the parking area onto a bench. Cross a flat, and continue to the junction with C297. Drive over a pass. From there, road C297 descends to a junction with C099. The latter runs into EF401 in 1.2 miles. Go left (southeast) to return to Irwin Road.

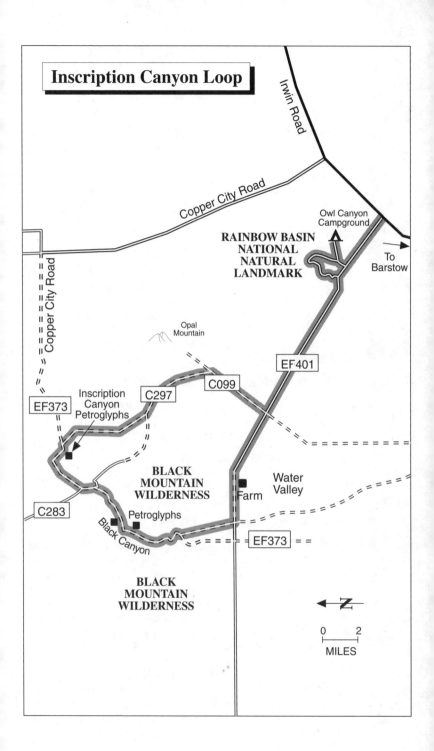

Inscription Canyon Loop

Irwin Road

Copper City Road

Copper City Road

Owl Canyon Campground

RAINBOW BASIN NATIONAL NATURAL LANDMARK

To Barstow

Opal Mountain

EF401

C099

C297

EF373

Inscription Canyon Petroglyphs

BLACK MOUNTAIN WILDERNESS

Water Valley

Farm

C283

Black Canyon

Petroglyphs

EF373

BLACK MOUNTAIN WILDERNESS

N

0   2
MILES

Afton Canyon

LOCATION: 37 miles northeast of Barstow; south of I-15. San Bernardino County.

HIGHLIGHTS: Colorful Afton Canyon's fluted walls rise some 300 feet above the Mojave River. It is thought to have been carved over time as Pleistocene Manix Lake drained through a rift in the earth caused by an earthquake some 15,000 years ago. Today, it is one of only three places where the river has surface flow below its headwaters during non-flood periods. The presence of surface water here during most of the year makes it critical wildlife habitat. Early in the drive you'll likely have a rare desert experience: fording water. The canyon was part of the historic Mojave Road (Tour 34).

DIFFICULTY: Easy to moderate. Follow the BLM's brown "Open Route" signs. Part of the route follows the bed of the Mojave River, which is sandy and can be treacherously soft when the weather's hot and dry. Air down to 15 psi or lower for better traction, and use established tracks. The sand bars may be best. Other sections run alongside the railroad tracks that parallel the river; don't linger there, because the rail line is busy. Stay out of the riverbed if it's flooded.

TIME & DISTANCE: 1.5 hours; 10 miles round-trip.

MAPS: BLM's *Soda Mountains* Desert Access Guide. ACSC's *San Bernardino County*. This was part of the old Mojave Road, so Dennis G. Casebier's book *Mojave Road Guide* is useful.

INFORMATION: BLM, Barstow Field Office.

GETTING THERE: From Barstow, take I-15 east for 37 miles. Take the Afton Road exit.

REST STOPS: The campground has water, tables, toilets.

THE DRIVE: Follow gravel Afton Canyon Road for 3.4 miles to the campground. From there, drive parallel to the riverbed for a mile, then pass under a railroad bridge and cross the riverbed. (You're likely to see a few freight trains on this drive.) As you enter the canyon, the railroad tracks will be on the left. The well-marked route winds along the tracks. 0.6 mile from the railroad bridge the route angles right, dipping into the riverbed. Here and there you might want to leave the riverbed and get close to the tracks, depending on conditions in the riverbed. Some road sections may be washed out, but there will be alternate tracks. At about mile 5 you will exit the canyon, and soon reach the Basin railroad siding. On the other side of the river is an old limestone mine. You can drive to it if the riverbed sand is fairly firm, and perhaps continue on to I-15 via Basin Road, but inspect the crossing first. The sand can be very soft. Afton Canyon is the point of the drive, anyway.

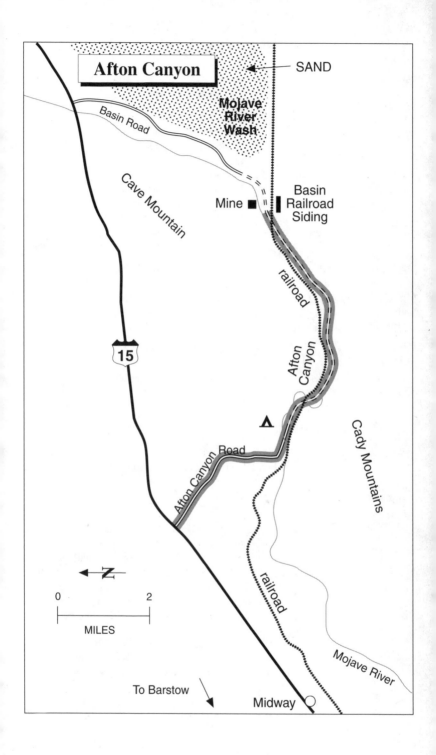

Afton Canyon

SAND

Mojave River Wash

Basin Road

Cave Mountain

Mine ■   ▌ Basin Railroad Siding

railroad

Afton Canyon

15

Afton Canyon Road

Cady Mountains

N

0   2

MILES

railroad

Mojave River

To Barstow

Midway ○

Aiken Mine Road

LOCATION: Mojave National Preserve; east of Baker. San Bernardino County.

HIGHLIGHTS: This tour, most of which is flanked by wilderness, follows Aiken Mine Road across the Cinder Cone Lava Beds, a volcanic landscape with dozens of vents, lava flows and cinder cones, and layers of volcanic rock (basalt) up to 400 feet thick. It was created by volcanic activity over millions of years, and as recently as 800 to 1,000 years ago. You also will see the vast Joshua tree forest that blankets Cima (Spanish for *summit*) Dome, a rounded landform that covers 75 square miles and rises 1,500 feet above the desert. It is thought to have formed when rising molten rock deep below the surface cooled, and was exposed by erosion.

DIFFICULTY: Easy, but there is a long stretch of soft sand at the north end that I rate moderately difficult. It will require airing down your tires (bring a small air compressor to reinflate them), and maintaining speed and momentum.

TIME & DISTANCE: 1.5 hours; 23.5 miles.

MAPS: ACSC's *San Bernardino County*. Trails Illustrated's *Mojave National Preserve* (No. 256). BLM's *Ivanpah* Desert Access Guide.

INFORMATION: Mojave National Preserve's Baker and Needles information centers.

GETTING THERE: From Baker, on I-15: Take Kelbaker Road southeast for 19.3 miles. Turn left onto Aiken Mine Road. **From Kelso:** Take Kelbaker Road northwest for 15.2 miles, then turn right.

REST STOPS: Anywhere that appeals to you.

THE DRIVE: The road takes you into a lonely expanse of lava rock, Joshua trees and cinder cones. It gradually climbs to a gap, from which you can gaze out at the Mojave Desert, and at mile 7 you will reach the Aiken cinder mine. Nailed to a pole should be a sign pointing left (north) to Cima Road, the way to go. At mile 10 are a corral, water tank and windmill. Stop here to air down your tires, to perhaps 15 psi, for better flotation on the sand ahead. At about mile 12.3 the road passes below power lines, then immediately bends left (northwest). (A smaller road continues east through the Joshua tree forest.) Rising to the east is Cima Dome. From here the road you will follow is straight for about 5.6 miles. By about mile 17.3 it becomes very sandy, so speed up and keep moving. In a couple of miles you will pass a residence. Beyond it the roadbed is firmer. At mile 23.5 you will come to paved Cima Road, just south of the interstate. Air up your tires here.

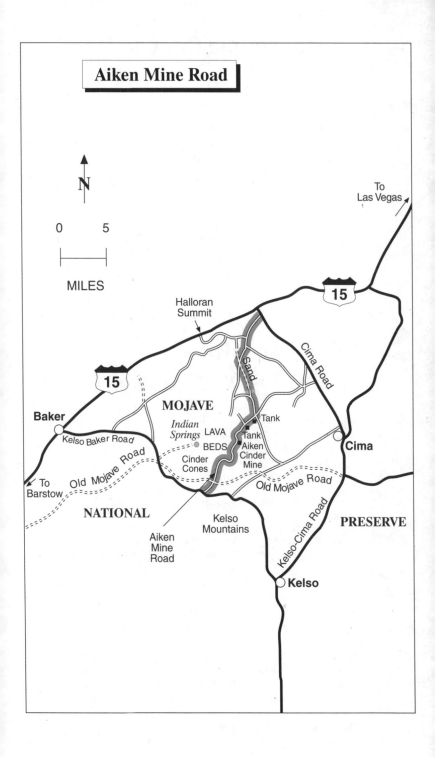

Aiken Mine Road

N

0   5

MILES

To Las Vegas

15

Halloran Summit

Sand

Cima Road

15

Baker

MOJAVE

Kelso Baker Road

Indian Springs

LAVA

Tank

Tank
Aiken
Cinder
Mine

Cima

BEDS

Cinder Cones

Old Mojave Road

Old Mojave Road

To Barstow

NATIONAL

Aiken Mine Road

Kelso Mountains

Kelso-Cima Road

PRESERVE

Kelso

Macedonia Canyon Road

LOCATION: Mojave National Preserve, between Wild Horse Canyon Road and Kelso-Cima Road. San Bernardino County.

HIGHLIGHTS: This is a short cruise down a wash in a low canyon between the Providence Mountains, to the south, and the Mid Hills, to the north. It provides fine vistas across broad, sloping valleys to distant mountain ranges. Getting to the route requires driving about half of Wild Horse Canyon Road (Tour 29). Watch out for desert tortoises, an endangered species and the California state reptile.

DIFFICULTY: Easy. You may have to dig out some sand from the railroad underpass at the end, so bring a shovel. The underpass is low, so check your roof's clearance.

TIME & DISTANCE: 40 minutes; 6.3 miles.

MAPS: ACSC's *San Bernardino County*. Trails Illustrated's *Mojave National Preserve* (No. 256). BLM's *Ivanpah* Desert Access Guide.

INFORMATION: MNP's Baker and Needles information centers. Hole-In-The-Wall Visitor Center, if it's open.

GETTING THERE: To go west (the way I describe)**:** The easy-to-miss entrance is midway along Wild Horse Canyon Road (Tour 29), on the west side of the road 5.7 miles from Wild Horse's north end and 5.9 miles from its south end. Watch for the signpost amid the pinyon-juniper woodland. Set your odometer to 0. **To go east:** The entrance is a tunnel beneath railroad tracks on the east side of Kelso-Cima Road, 8 miles northeast of Kelso.

REST STOPS: There is a picnic area at the visitor center at Hole-In-The-Wall. A campground is nearby as well. Mid Hills Campground is higher, cooler and woodsy.

THE DRIVE: After you've passed through a gate, the route begins a gradual but steady descent down a wash of granitic sand amid rocky hills, pinyon pines, junipers and spiney yucca plants. On either side are numerous fractured granite boulders. The canyon's low walls form a gunsight of sorts ahead, framing a distant view of the Shadow and Marl mountains as well as 1,500-foot-tall Cima Dome. A number of old mine sites still scar the hills here. At mile 2.6 is the junction with the spur to Macedonia Spring and the inactive Columbia Mine, to the left (south). Go right. You're out of the canyon now, and from here the road descends toward the Union Pacific tracks and paved Kelso-Cima Road. I passed right over a desert tortoise here once, thinking it was just a rock. I stopped, saw what it was, and moved it well off the road, apparently unharmed. It was a reminder that as lifeless as deserts can appear to be, they are in fact full of life. Soon you will reach the railroad underpass. Kelso-Cima Road lies just beyond.

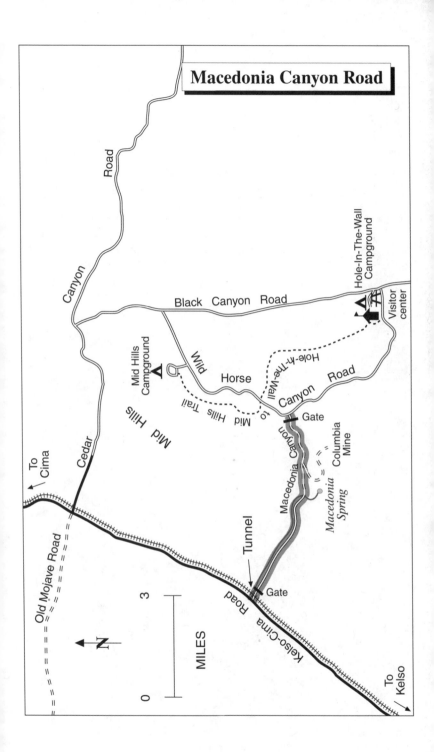

Macedonia Canyon Road

Road

Canyon

Canyon

Black Canyon Road

Hole-In-The-Wall Campground

Visitor center

Mid Hills Campground

Wild

Horse

Hole-in-The-Wall

Canyon Road

Mid Hills Trail

Mid Hills

Gate

Cedar

Macedonia Canyon

Columbia Mine

To Cima

Macedonia Spring

Tunnel

Old Mojave Road

Gate

3

N

Kelso-Cima Road

MILES

0

To Kelso

85

Desert tortoise, Macedonia Canyon Road *(Tour 28)*

Kelso Depot, Mojave National Preserve

Wild Horse Canyon

LOCATION: Mojave National Preserve. San Bernardino County.

HIGHLIGHTS: This road was designated a National Back Country Byway during the time of the BLM-managed East Mojave Scenic Area, predecessor of today's national preserve, which the National Park Service manages. Getting to the route, you'll drive through magnificent high-desert scenery, past Wild Horse Mesa and the colorful volcanic formations at Hole-In-The-Wall. The road connects to Macedonia Canyon Road (Tour 28) about midway through, and Black Canyon Road (Tour 30) at either end.

DIFFICULTY: This is an easy loop, but flash floods in summer can make the route impassable.

TIME & DISTANCE: 45 minutes; 11.7 miles.

MAPS: ACSC's *San Bernardino County*. Trails Illustrated's *Mojave National Preserve* (No. 256). BLM's *Ivanpah* Desert Access Guide.

INFORMATION: Mojave National Preserve's Baker and Needles information centers. The Hole-In-The-Wall Visitor Center, if it's open.

GETTING THERE: Wild Horse Canyon Road is west of Black Canyon Road and Hole-In-The-Wall. The north end is 2.8 miles south of Cedar Canyon Road. The south end is about 12.7 miles north of I-40 via Essex Road and Black Canyon Road. You can take the drive in either direction.

REST STOPS: Mid Hills and Hole-In-The-Wall campgrounds have water. Mid Hills is woodsy, higher and cooler. An 8-mile hiking trail descends from Mid Hills Campground to Wild Horse Canyon Road, passing through cactus gardens and rock formations. Explore the volcanic formations at Hole-In-The-Wall, and don't miss the short Ring Trail hike there, which involves scrambling down rock chutes via metal rings imbedded in the rock.

THE DRIVE: Here, at about 5,400 feet, this high-desert backway passes through rolling, rocky hills of granite and volcanic rock covered with sagebrush, pinyon pine and juniper. Along its undulating course are some of the best vistas across the eastern Mojave Desert, including the jagged peaks of the Providence Mountains, Kelso Sand Dunes and Devil's Playground. Near the southern end, a mile west of Hole-In-The-Wall campground, it even passes through a cactus garden.

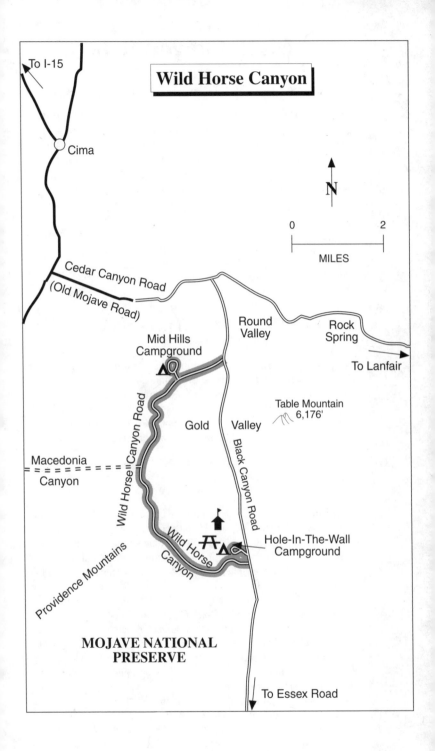

Wild Horse Canyon

To I-15

Cima

N

0   2
MILES

Cedar Canyon Road
(Old Mojave Road)

Round
Valley

Rock
Spring

To Lanfair

Mid Hills
Campground

Table Mountain
6,176'

Gold   Valley

Wild Horse Canyon Road

Black Canyon Road

Macedonia
Canyon

Wild Horse
Canyon

Hole-In-The-Wall
Campground

Providence Mountains

MOJAVE NATIONAL
PRESERVE

To Essex Road

Black Canyon Road

LOCATION: Mojave National Preserve. San Bernardino County.

HIGHLIGHTS: This backway was designated a National Back Country Byway during the time of the BLM-managed East Mojave Scenic Area, predecessor of today's national preserve, which the National Park Service manages. It takes in spectacular high-desert vistas, spring wildflowers and the fascinating volcanic formations at Hole-In-The-Wall. There are fine views of Table Mountain, the Providence Mountains, Woods Mountains and Colton Hills as well.

DIFFICULTY: This is an easy cruise on a maintained 2WD road that is subject to flash floods.

TIME & DISTANCE: 30 minutes; 17 miles.

MAPS: ACSC's *San Bernardino County*. Trails Illustrated's *Mojave National Preserve* (No. 256).

INFORMATION: Mojave National Preserve's Baker and Needles information centers.

GETTING THERE: I describe this from north to south. Find your way to Kelso-Cima Road in Mojave National Preserve, between I-15 and I-40 east of Barstow. From Kelso-Cima Road, take Cedar Canyon Road (Tour 31) east for 4.5 miles, to the turnoff (south) for Black Canyon Road. To go north, from I-40, exit at Essex Road. Follow Essex Road northwest for 9.7 miles, then go north on Black Canyon Road.

REST STOPS: Mid Hills Campground. Also Hole-In-The-Wall Campground, picnic area and visitor center. Mitchell Caverns and Providence Mountains State Recreation Area.

THE DRIVE: You begin at Cedar Canyon, at about 5,000 feet elevation in the Mid Hills, and immediately cross Cedar Wash. From there the road gradually climbs about 300 feet through pinyon pine, juniper, sagebrush and hills strewn with granite boulders. In 2.8 miles you will see the turnoff, on the right (west) for Mid Hills Campground and the north end of Wild Horse Canyon Road (Tour 29), which is also the access road for Macedonia Canyon Road (Tour 28). About a mile south of Wild Horse Canyon Road, Black Canyon Road enters its namesake. Now you're getting views of Table Mountain, distant ranges and broad desert valleys. When you reach the turnoff for Hole-In-The-Wall, take time to view the spectacularly eroded volcanic rock there. Continuing south, a panorama, beautiful in late afternoon light, opens up before you as the road makes a long descent. Speed can creep up on you on these gradual, steady descents, so be careful. Watch out for cattle on the road, too. Soon you will see the glint of the modern world as, far off in the distance, traffic moves along I-40 amid a primeval desert landscape. At Essex Road, Mitchell Caverns will be 6 miles to the right, I-40 10 miles to the left.

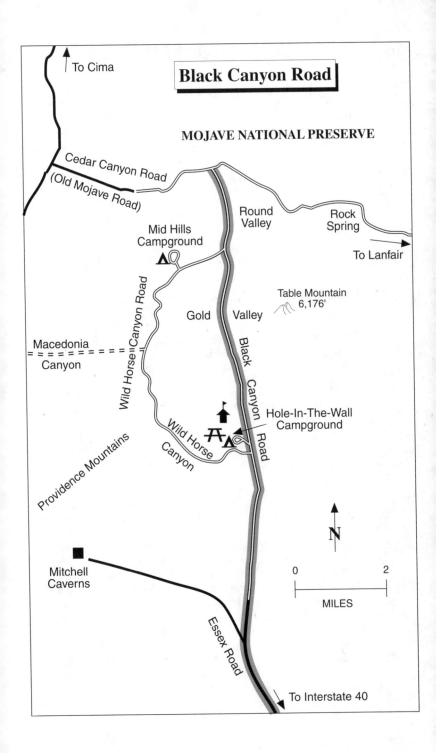

Cedar Canyon Road

LOCATION: Mojave National Preserve. San Bernardino County.

HIGHLIGHTS: This east-west road, designated a National Back Country Byway when the BLM managed the desert here (it's now managed by the National Park Service), goes through the geographic center of the Mojave Desert. The road either follows or parallels much of the old Mojave Road (Tour 34).

DIFFICULTY: Easy, on a maintained dirt-and-gravel road that is subject to floods during late-summer storms.

TIME & DISTANCE: 30 minutes; 19.3 miles.

MAPS: ACSC's *San Bernardino County*. Trails Illustrated's *Mojave National Preserve* (No. 256).

INFORMATION: Mojave National Preserve's Baker and Needles information centers.

GETTING THERE: From Baker, on I-15, take Kelbaker Road 34.5 miles southeast to Kelso. From Kelso, take Kelso-Cima Road 14.4 miles northeast. Turn right (east) onto to Cedar Canyon Road.

REST STOPS: Mid Hills and Hole-In-The-Wall campgrounds (the former is higher, cooler and wooded, with terrific vistas; the latter is near fascinating volcanic formations and the visitor center). Petroglyphs and old Army graffiti can be seen in the Rock Spring area, a popular place for primitive camping. Camp at least a quarter-mile from the spring.

THE DRIVE: Cedar Canyon Road climbs from Ivanpah Valley into the Mid Hills, which are wooded with pinyon pines and junipers and strewn with granite boulders. In 2.5 miles the pavement ends and the graded dirt-and-gravel road begins. Before you enter Cedar Canyon, stop and look back the vast panorama of the eastern Mojave. Soon you will descend into the canyon, where the road narrows. 6 miles from the start is the junction with Black Canyon Road (Tour 30). It would take you to Wild Horse Canyon Road (Tour 29), and to campgrounds at Mid Hills (5 miles) and Hole-In-The-Wall (10 miles). From here the road winds through desert hills. To the north are Pinto Mountain and the peaks of the New York Mountains. South of the road, where it crosses Watson Wash just over 5 miles east of Black Canyon Road, is Rock Spring, a watering hole along the old Mojave Road that also was used by Indians for thousands of years. The U.S. Army established an outpost there in 1866. It was considered one of the Army's most isolated and primitive posts, and it closed after a little more than a year. Still standing near the old camp, just beyond the south side of the road, is a stone house built in 1929 by World War I gas victim Bert Smith. He died in 1954. The road ends at Ivanpah-Lanfair Road (Tour 33).

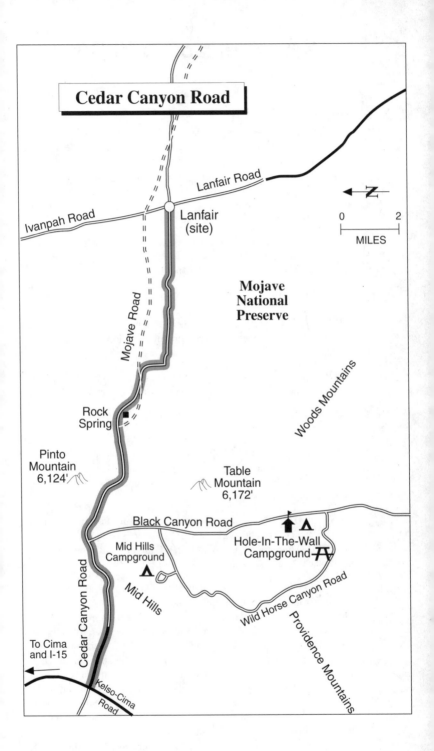

Cedar Canyon Road

New York Mountain Road

LOCATION: Mojave National Preserve. San Bernardino County.

HIGHLIGHTS: Rising to 7,500 feet, the craggy New York Mountains are an intriguing contrast to the broad, sloping landscapes of the Mojave Desert. The mountains, largely granite, include Precambrian igneous and metamorphic rock as old as 1 billion years. Uniquely, oaks and white firs have a foothold in these mountains, which are noted as well for a series of volcanic spires, Castle Peaks (northeast of this drive). Caruthers Canyon, where a stream winds through a jumble of granite boulders amid chaparral, is not to be missed.

DIFFICULTY: Most of the route is easy. However, while Caruthers Canyon is easy for the first two miles or so, it becomes rocky (moderate to difficult) thereafter. Boulder-strewn and eroded toward the end, it eventually is reduced to a foot trail. Park when the going gets rough, then walk.

TIME & DISTANCE: 2.5 hours; about 16.6 miles. But you can spend considerably more time and cover more miles exploring the area if you wish.

MAPS: ACSC's *San Bernardino County*. BLM's *Ivanpah* Desert Access Guide. Trails Illustrated's *Mojave National Preserve* (No. 256).

INFORMATION: Mojave National Preserve's Baker and Needles information centers.

GETTING THERE: At MNP, make your way to Ivanpah Road. New York Mountain Road begins on the west side of Ivanpah Road, 5.3 miles north of the junction with Cedar Canyon and Lanfair roads. Set your odometer to 0 here.

REST STOPS: There are good primitive campsites in Caruthers Canyon, which is at about 5,500 feet. High, woodsy and relatively cool Mid Hills Campground, off Wild Horse Canyon Road (Tour 29), is a great place for a base camp.

THE DRIVE: New York Mountain Road climbs gradually through a mix of Joshua trees, pinyon pines and junipers, with the New York Mountains rising ever higher as you approach them. At mile 5.5 is a 4-way junction. Go right (north), and follow the road directly up Caruthers Canyon. Avoid the spurs that branch off the main road, which becomes smaller and rockier. I suggest parking by about mile 7.7. If you find old mines interesting, it's about a 20-minute hike to the Giant Ledge copper mine. (Abandoned mines are dangerous. Stay out of the tunnels.) Back at the 4-way junction, go right (west), and drive along the mountains for 3.1 miles. You should see a small two-track branching off to the left here; take it. You will cross Watson Wash and arrive at the north-south road through Pinto Valley in about 0.6 mile. Go left (south) there. In 3.6 miles you'll arrive at Cedar Canyon Road (Tour 31).

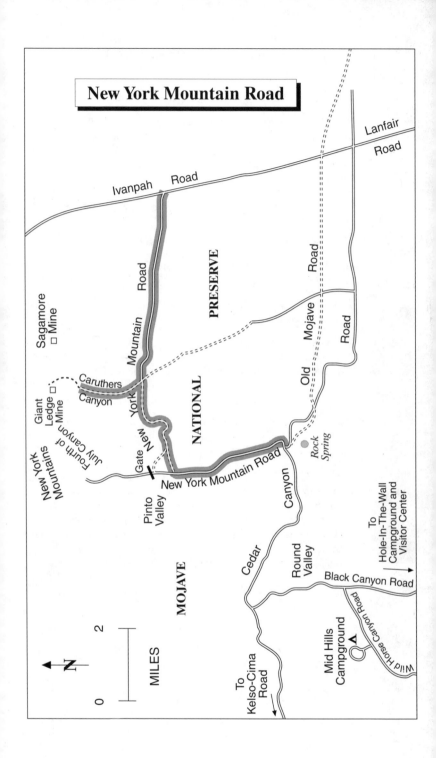

New York Mountain Road

Ivanpah-Lanfair Road

LOCATION: Mojave National Preserve. San Bernardino County.

HIGHLIGHTS: This road, designated a BLM National Back Country Byway when this region was under the BLM's management (it's now under the National Park Service) provides fabulous high-desert scenery, including the New York Mountains, Castle Peaks, Lanfair Valley and Hackberry Mountains.

DIFFICULTY: Easy 2WD. The first and final few miles are paved. The rest is graded dirt. Floods are possible.

TIME & DISTANCE: 1.5 hours; 45 miles from Goffs to Nipton Road.

MAPS: ACSC's *San Bernardino County*. Trails Illustrated's *Mojave National Preserve* (No. 256).

INFORMATION: Mojave National Preserve's Baker and Needles information centers.

GETTING THERE: From I-15: Take the Nipton Road exit. Drive about 3.5 miles east, then turn right (south) onto Ivanpah Road. **From I-40:** Take the Goffs Road exit. Drive northeast 10.4 miles to Goffs. Go northwest on Lanfair Road.

REST STOPS: Beautiful Caruthers Canyon, in the New York Mountains (see Tour 32) has good primitive campsites. There are developed campgrounds at Hole-In-The-Wall and Mid Hills, both off Black Canyon Road (Tour 30).

THE DRIVE: From either direction, you'll climb steadily on this north-south road, from below 3,000 feet elevation to more than 5,000 feet in the beautiful New York Mountains, along the northern section. You'll cross Fenner and Lanfair valleys, look out at the rugged ridges and peaks of the Hackberry Mountains, the Vontrigger Hills, the Castle Mountains and the volcanic spires of Castle Peaks, a popular hiking destination. Almost 16 miles north of Goffs, you will come to the inter-section with Cedar Canyon Road (Tour 31). 5.3 miles north of that, New York Mountain Road (Tour 32) will be on the left.

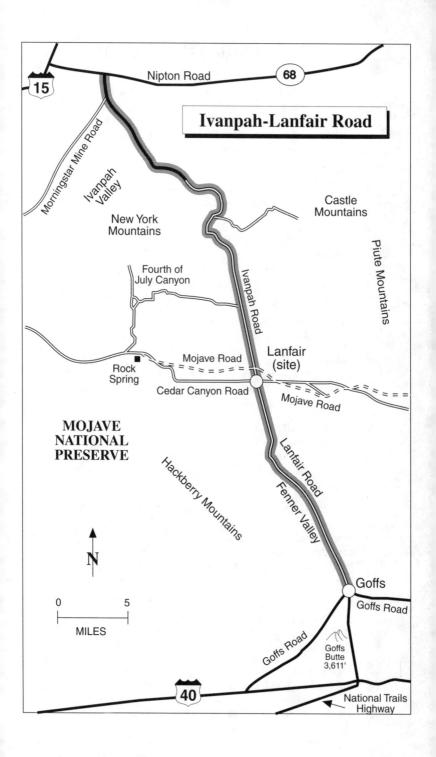

Ivanpah-Lanfair Road

Mojave Road

LOCATION: It begins on the west bank of the Colorado River in Nevada at the Fort Mojave Indian Reservation north of Needles, Calif., and passes through Mojave National Preserve. It ends east of Barstow on I-15, at Manix near the site of the 19th century Army outpost, Camp Cady. San Bernardino County.

HIGHLIGHTS: You will not only travel an often remote and historic desert road, but you'll encounter such scenic desert gems as Mojave National Preserve and Afton Canyon. There also are historic ruins, rock art and interesting geologic sites.

DIFFICULTY: Easy to moderate, and potentially difficult. There are stretches that can be treacherously sandy or muddy, including Soda Lake, the Mojave River flood plain and Afton Canyon. You may have to detour around them. If you drive the entire road, go with a party of several vehicles for safety.

TIME & DISTANCE: 2-3 days if you drive the entire 138-mile route. You can also just drive segments of it.

MAPS: Mojave National Preserve has a map, adapted from the ACSC's *San Bernardino County* map, that depicts much of the route. Also bring the BLM's *Needles*, *Ivanpah*, *Soda Mountains* and *Newberry Springs* Desert Access Guides.

INFORMATION: Mojave National Preserve's Baker and Needles information centers. Friends of the Mojave Road. Don't go without the book *Mojave Road Guide: An Adventure Through Time*, by Dennis G. Casebier and Friends of the Mojave Road. It is the definitive guide to the route.

GETTING THERE: The road can be taken in segments from a number of points in the region. (Refer to your maps.) From the bridge over I-40 at Needles: Take River Road/Needles Highway north toward Laughlin, Nevada. In about 15.7 miles go left (west) onto the Mojave Road. (Purists can begin at the road's true starting point, 3 miles east of the highway on the Fort Mojave Indian Reservation, at the Colorado River.)

REST STOPS: Mojave National Preserve's Mid Hills and Hole-In-The-Wall campgrounds have water. There are primitive campsites along the way as well.

THE DRIVE: This historic road began as an Indian trail with reliable sources of water. From explorers like Jedediah Smith to prospectors and Army troops, all sorts of people who moved West in the 1800s used it. In the 1980s it was restored for public use by author and historian Dennis Casebier and the Friends of the Mojave Road. It climbs from under 500 feet elevation at the start to over 5,000 feet in Mojave National Preserve. Along the way it passes a rich variety of desert vegetation as well as historic sites like the rock remains of an 1860s Army outpost, Fort Piute, and prehistoric sites with ancient petroglyphs.

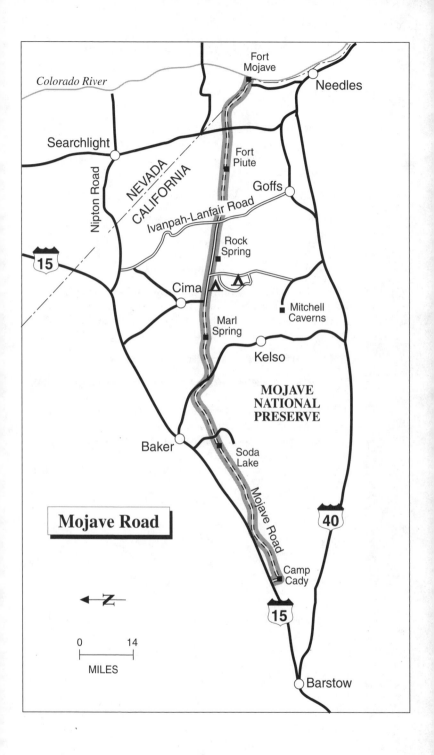

Mojave Road

Stoddard Well Road

LOCATION: Between Victorville and Barstow. San Bernardino County.

HIGHLIGHTS: Stoddard Well (also Wells) Road provides vistas of a vast desert landscape of volcanic mountains and broad, sloping valleys, making this an appealing and relaxing desert cruise and a great alternative to the freeways.

DIFFICULTY: The graded dirt road couldn't be easier.

TIME & DISTANCE: 1 hour; about 23 miles.

MAP: ACSC's *San Bernardino County*.

INFORMATION: BLM's Barstow Field Office.

GETTING THERE: From I-15 north of Victorville: Take the Stoddard Wells Road exit. **From Barstow:** Take Barstow Road (Hwy. 247) south about 6 miles, then turn right (west) onto Stoddard Well Road.

REST STOPS: Victorville and Barstow have all services.

THE DRIVE: If you're looking for an easy cruise through beautiful desert, this is it. Going from Victorville, the road parallels I-15 for about 3.5 miles, then veers northeast. The pavement ends after about 7.6 miles, and 2.5 miles later you're in the desert hills and mountains, and then Stoddard Valley. The road passes through the 33,500-acre Stoddard Valley Off-Highway Vehicle Area, where cross-country driving is allowed. You'll see the scars. When you reach Barstow Road, go left (north).

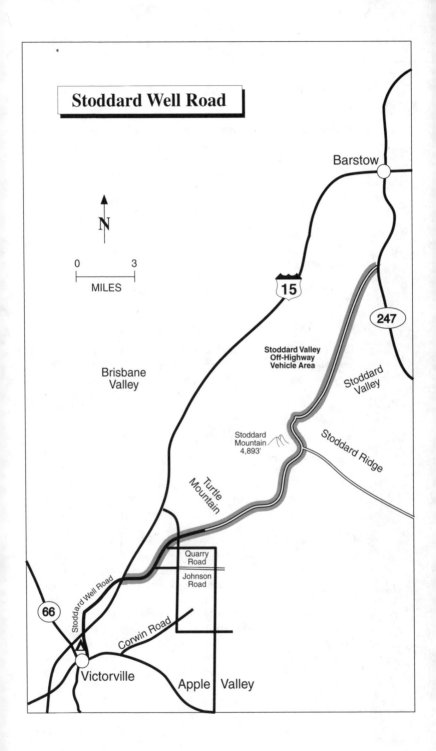

Camp Rock Road

LOCATION: Between Lucerne Valley and I-40 east of Barstow. San Bernardino County.

HIGHLIGHTS: This relaxing sojourn provides fine views of several desert mountain ranges and the broad, sloping valleys that lie between them. You can add short side trips to craggy Cougar Buttes, at the south end, and the Surprise Tank petroglyphs farther north.

DIFFICULTY: Easy. Camp Rock Road is largely a graded 2WD road. 10.2 miles of it north of Hwy. 247 are paved. The road to Surprise Tank, part of the Rodman Mountains Loop (Tour 37) is more rudimentary.

TIME & DISTANCE: 2.5 hours; about 51 miles with sidetrips. You can go in either direction, north or south.

MAPS: ACSC's *San Bernardino County*. BLM's *Newberry Springs* Desert Access Guide.

INFORMATION: BLM's Barstow Field Office.

GETTING THERE: From Victorville, the way I describe the drive: Take Hwy. 18 to Lucerne Valley; continue east on Hwy. 247. Where Hwy. 247 angles southeast, Camp Rock Road goes north. (Set your odomenter to 0 here.) 3.7 miles from Hwy. 247, Camp Rock Road angles northeast. **From Barstow:** Take I-40 east 5.6 miles. Exit at Daggett, and turn right. Turn left (east) onto Pendleton Road (which becomes Camp Rock Road when the pavement ends).

REST STOPS: Anywhere you find appealing.

THE DRIVE: As the road takes you into the region's volcanic hills, you will soon see a jagged cluster of rocks to the east, Cougar Buttes, which are worth visiting. To do so, turn right (east) at Cambria Road. Camp Rock Road eventually will bend to the right (northeast), and Harrod Road will continue north. The road will take you between the Ord Mountains, to the west, and the Fry Mountains, to the east. The Johnson Valley Off-Highway Vehicle Area lies east of the road as well. At about mile 20, at the junction with road 0J228 (Cinder Cone Road), Camp Rock Road goes left (northwest). But you can turn right (east) and follow 0J288 for 6.8 miles toward a cinder mine. Just before the mine, turn right again, onto road OJ233. In 1.1 mile, just after passing through a ravine, you will see a left fork from the main road. It goes to two fenced areas that protect ancient geoglyphs (see Tour 37), rocks deliberately arranged on the ground to form a shape, and to a ravine, Surprise Tank. There you can view Indian petroglyphs, some of which may be as old as 11,000 years. Common are zigzags thought to have been created by rattlesnake shamans of the Vanyume people. Back at Camp Rock Road, drive northwest along the edge of the Newberry Mountains Wilderness to reach I-40 in 18 miles.

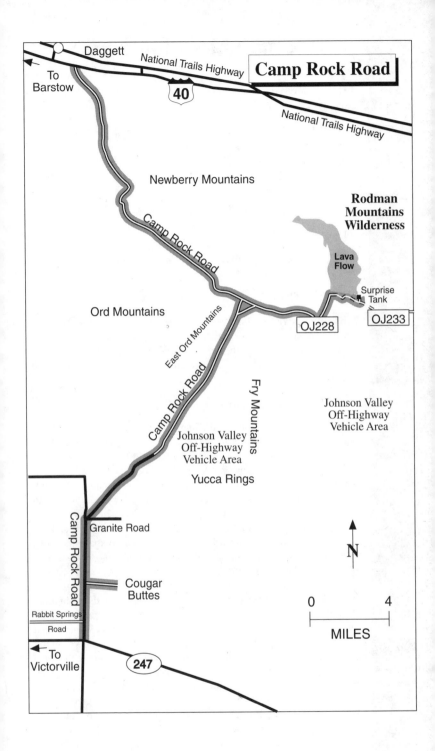

Rodman Mountains Loop

LOCATION: South of I-40, southeast of Barstow. San Bernardino County.

HIGHLIGHTS: The prehistoric rock art and geoglyphs (ground designs created in the desert pavement) at Surprise Tank are fascinating. You will also drive down Box Canyon, a narrow, rock-walled corridor that separates the eastern and western sections of the Rodman Mountains Wilderness, where mechanized travel is prohibited.

DIFFICULTY: Easy to moderate. Expect sandy stretches.

TIME & DISTANCE: 4 hours; 40 miles.

MAPS: ACSC's *San Bernardino County*. BLM's *Newberry Springs* Desert Access Guide.

INFORMATION: BLM's Barstow Field Office.

GETTING THERE: Take I-40 southeast for 5.6 miles from the eastern edge of Barstow. Take the Daggett/A Street exit, and go right. In a short distance go left (southeast) on paved Pendleton Road, which soon becomes unpaved Camp Rock Road (Tour 36). Set your odometer at 0 at pavement's end.

REST STOPS: Almost anywhere.

THE DRIVE: The graded road climbs into rolling hills and through a small canyon, and then into a valley between the Newberry and Ord Mountains. At mile 17.1 Camp Rock Road turns to the southwest. Go straight, onto Cinder Cone Road (OJ228). After another mile go left. Just as you approach the cinder mine, take a small dirt road on the right, OJ233. In about 1.1 miles, just beyond a ravine, the road will fork to the right. To the left, toward the Rodman Mountains, are two fenced areas protecting prehistoric Indian geoglyphs. The first is what appears to be a ram's horns. The site also includes an ancient footpath that looks like a motorcycle track. The second area protects a shape that might be likened to a large boomerang. A short distance to the southeast is a basalt ravine, the Surprise Tank petroglyph site. (In the desert, a "tank" is a rock area that collects water.) It's best to continue on the main route 0.8 mile farther, and go left on a two-track to a parking area at the south end of the tank, and then tour the site. Scan the arroyo's walls, which bear some 900 petroglyphs. Some may be as old as 11,000 years, but most are thought to be less than 1,000 years old. Common are zigzags believed to have been created by rattlesnake shamans of the Vanyume people to symbolize their spirit helpers. 2.5 miles farther, at a junction, go left, under the power lines, then left again in 0.4 mile onto OJ295. It will take you into Box Canyon, then onto a slope overlooking I-40. Follow the wash to the gas pipeline road, then go left (west). In 1.6 miles go right (north). Continue to National Trails Highway and I-40.

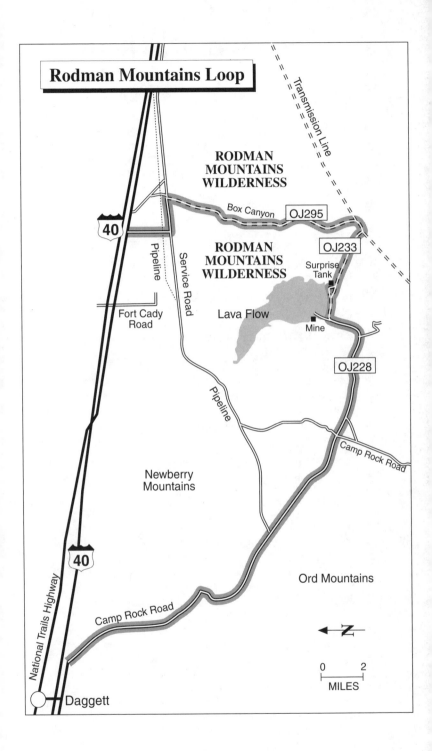

Rodman Mountains Loop

RODMAN MOUNTAINS WILDERNESS

Transmission Line

Box Canyon OJ295

OJ233

RODMAN MOUNTAINS WILDERNESS

Surprise Tank

Lava Flow

Mine

OJ228

Pipeline

Service Road

Fort Cady Road

Pipeline

Newberry Mountains

Camp Rock Road

Ord Mountains

Camp Rock Road

National Trails Highway

Daggett

0   2
MILES

Burns Canyon Road

LOCATION: Between Yucca Valley and Baldwin Lake. San Bernardino County.

HIGHLIGHTS: The scenery will vary with the changing life zones this tour traverses, as you climb from about 4,140 feet elevation in the Mojave Desert to as high as 7,300 feet into the forested San Bernardino Mountains. Burns Canyon is beautiful, and you'll see giant Joshua trees as well.

DIFFICULTY: Easy.

TIME & DISTANCE: 4 hours; about 27 miles.

MAPS: ACSC's *San Bernardino County*. San Bernardino National Forest.

INFORMATION: San Bernardino National Forest, Big Bear Ranger District.

GETTING THERE: From the Palm Springs area: Take Hwy. 62 northeast from I-10 for about 19.5 miles, to the western end of Yucca Valley. Then take Pioneertown Road northwest toward Pipes Canyon Road, but go straight onto Rimrock Road instead. It will make a sharp bend to the left. In 0.8 mile the pavement ends. Set your odometer to 0 here. **From the north:** Take Hwy. 247 southeast beyond Flamingo Heights. Go west on Pipes Canyon Road for 6.6 miles, then right onto Rimrock Road.

REST STOPS: There are places along the way, particularly at the Rose Mine area. Big Bear Lake has all services.

THE DRIVE: Pass through a residential area and dense Joshua tree forest (the big ones come later), then continue up Burns Canyon on Burns Canyon Road, crossing a wash several times. The road forks about 4.9 miles from the end of the pavement. Go right, following the orange arrows on the Joshua trees. At about mile 6 is an intersection. Go left, toward Big Bear City. 0.4 mile farther the road to Mound Spring and the large Joshua trees branches right (north). You will see the Farrington Observatory off to the right, then cross a cattle guard. Now you're on road 3N06. Veer left, and the road will take you into a valley with huge Joshua trees. Retrace your route to continue northeast on Burns Canyon Road. Soon you will enter San Bernardino National Forest, climbing steeply through mountains of fractured granite, and the road becomes No. 2N02. About 4.4 miles from where you rejoined the main road after visiting the Joshua trees is an intersection, at the old Rose Mine. You can go straight, and take road 3N03 for 8.5 miles through Lone Valley to Hwy. 18, but the more scenic route is to go left (south) and follow 2N01 (Round Valley Road) for 6 miles to Hwy. 38.

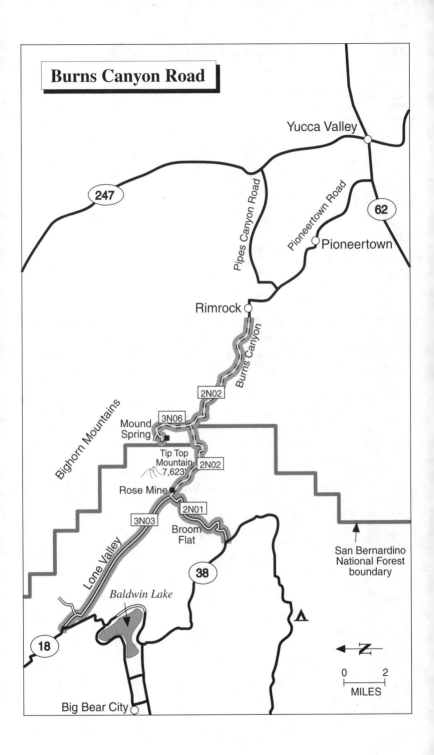

Burns Canyon Road

Yucca Valley

247

Pipes Canyon Road

Pioneertown Road

62

Pioneertown

Rimrock

Burns Canyon

2N02

3N06

Bighorn Mountains

Mound Spring

Tip Top Mountain 7,623'

2N02

Rose Mine

2N01

3N03

Broom Flat

38

Lone Valley

San Bernardino National Forest boundary

Baldwin Lake

18

N

0   2
MILES

Big Bear City

Covington Flats

LOCATION: Joshua Tree National Park. San Bernardino and Riverside counties.

HIGHLIGHTS: The dirt roads in Covington Flats provide access to some of the park's largest Joshua trees, as well as some of the lushest desert vegetation in the area's high desert. The vista from the summit of 5,516-foot Eureka Peak is outstanding.

DIFFICULTY: Easy.

TIME & DISTANCE: 1.5 hours; 21.6 miles round-trip.

MAPS: The park brochure is adequate, but you might also bring ACSC's *Riverside County* or Trails Illustrated's *Joshua Tree National Park* (No. 226).

INFORMATION: Joshua Tree National Park.

GETTING THERE: From Yucca Valley, drive 2.7 miles east on Hwy. 62 from the junction at Hwy. 247. Turn south on La Contenta Road, going about a mile and straight across Yucca Trail. Set your odometer at 0.

REST STOPS: There is a picnic area, but Eureka Peak is hard to beat.

THE DRIVE: Heading south, you will pass through a residential area, then angle left as you pass Joshua trees and cacti. At mile 7.7 the picnic area is directly ahead. Turn right (southwest), go another 1.8 miles, turn right (north) again, and after a steep climb you will arrive at Eureka Peak. From here you will have a view westward of the Palm Springs area, the Little San Bernardino Mountains and the Morongo Basin. The road southeast of the viewpoint goes to Upper Covington Flat, a wilderness trailhead and, a short hike from the end of the road, the park's largest known Joshua tree.

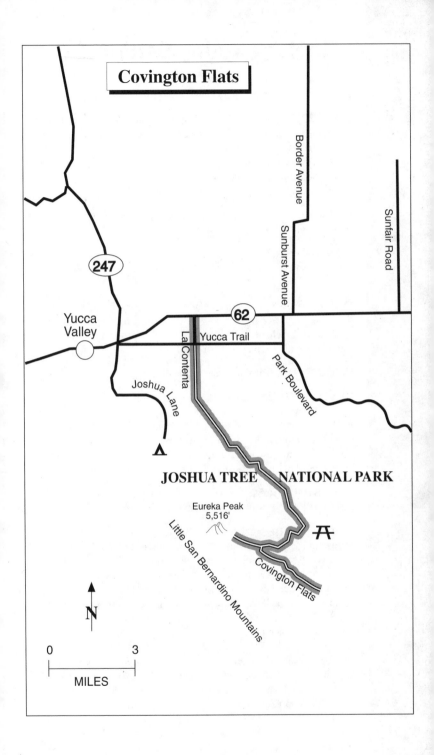

Covington Flats

Border Avenue

Sunfair Road

247

Sunburst Avenue

Yucca Valley

62

La Contenta

Yucca Trail

Park Boulevard

Joshua Lane

JOSHUA TREE   NATIONAL PARK

Eureka Peak
5,516'

Little San Bernardino Mountains

Covington Flats

N

0   3
MILES

Geology Tour—Berdoo Cyn.

LOCATION: Joshua Tree National Park. Riverside County.

HIGHLIGHTS: In a single drive, this self-guiding tour is a chance to see and learn about the park's complex geology and its human history. It connects to Berdoo Canyon Road, a more rugged 4WD route south to I-10. Berdoo Canyon occupies a biological melting pot, or transition zone, where the high Mojave Desert and the low Colorado Desert meet, and plants and animals from both deserts coexist.

DIFFICULTY: Easy, but conditions can change. Berdoo Canyon Road is moderately difficult and subject to washouts.

TIME & DISTANCE: 2 hours; 17.1 miles. Berdoo Canyon Road is 1.5 hours and 15.3 miles from the Geology Tour Road south to Dillon Road.

MAPS: ACSC's *Riverside County*, the park's map or Trails Illustrated's *Joshua Tree National Park* (No. 226). Get a copy of the interpretive brochure *Geology and Man* (25 cents) from the brown metal box at the starting point of the drive.

INFORMATION: Joshua Tree National Park.

GETTING THERE: From the towns of Joshua Tree or Twentynine Palms, both on Hwy. 62 north of the national park, head toward Jumbo Rocks Campground. If you're coming from the south, take I-10 to the Cottonwood Spring Road exit, drive north through the park's southern entrance and make your way toward Jumbo Rocks. The starting point for the drive is 1.6 miles west of the turnoff to Jumbo Rocks.

REST STOPS: Refer to your maps for campground locations in the park. You'll find toilets at Squaw Tank.

THE DRIVE: The brochure available at the starting point describes 16 points along the drive, which includes a one-way loop. For the first 4 miles you'll pass among massive boulders and rolling hills in Queen Valley. At mile 5.4 is the pullout for Squaw Tank. Native Americans inhabited the area from about 1000 A.D. to the turn of the 20th century, and Squaw Tank was a favorite spot. In the desert, the term "tank" often refers to a natural basin that collects rain water. At Squaw Tank you will see concrete dams that ranchers built to hold water for cattle in the early 1900s. There are petroglyphs, and bowl-like bedrock mortars that Indians used to grind seeds and other foods into meal. The road forks just beyond Squaw Tank; keep left, making your way across a dry lakebed via a loop road. (Turn back if it's wet.) At about mile 7.8, where the loop road angles right (west), you will see the left (south) turn to Berdoo Canyon Road. Keep to the right to continue the Geology Tour. Berdoo Canyon Road descends about 3,400 feet through a rugged and scenic canyon to reach Dillon Road, north of I-10, but it may be washed out so check in advance.

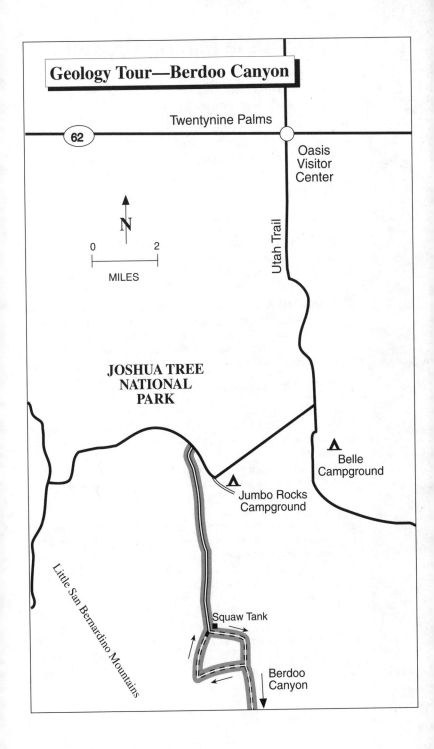

Geology Tour—Berdoo Canyon

Old Dale Mining District

LOCATION: Joshua Tree National Park and adjacent areas. San Bernardino and Riverside counties.

HIGHLIGHTS: The remains of the Dale gold-mining district are interesting, and you'll enjoy the vistas of Pinto Basin, especially in the light of late afternoon. A number of side roads lead to old mines and residences.

DIFFICULTY: Easy.

TIME & DISTANCE: At least 1.5 hours; 23 miles.

MAPS: ACSC's *Riverside County*, the park's brochure or Trails Illustrated's *Joshua Tree National Park* (No. 226).

INFORMATION: Joshua Tree National Park.

GETTING THERE: You can take this basically north-south drive in either direction. I describe it going south. Take Hwy. 62 east for 14.2 miles from the turnoff to the park at Twentynine Palms. Turn right (south) onto Gold Crown Road. If you'd rather travel north, the Old Dale Road turnoff is 6.8 miles northeast of Cottonwood Visitor Center.

REST STOPS: Just about anywhere that's appealing.

THE DRIVE: Set your odometer at 0 when you turn off Hwy. 62. This is the site of Old Dale, once a mining camp that sprouted after gold was discovered in the region in the early 1880s. (There are two more Dales to come.) Gold Crown Road is a good, wide dirt road. Follow it a bit more than 4.5 miles to Virginia Dale Mine, east of the road. It was founded in 1885, and a second Dale grew up around it. In the early 1900s, a gold discovery at the site of Supply Mine, 2 miles east, prompted folks to relocate the town. This third Dale, named New Dale, was located east of the main road where it turns sharply southwest. In a bit more than 2 miles the route goes left (southeast). Drive about 4 miles up into the Pinto Mountains, passing old mine sites, rubbish and private residences. The one-lane road, which becomes Old Dale Road, is rough in spots, but there shouldn't be a problem. Soon you will begin the beautiful descent into Pinto Basin, in the park. The road will cross an ecological transition zone as it leaves the Mojave Desert behind and enters the Colorado Desert. The vista is stunning in late afternoon's golden light and shadows. A half-mile before the dirt road widens, it will take you past the remains of Mission Well. It provided water to local mines and mills in the 1930s. The paved road is 9 miles farther.

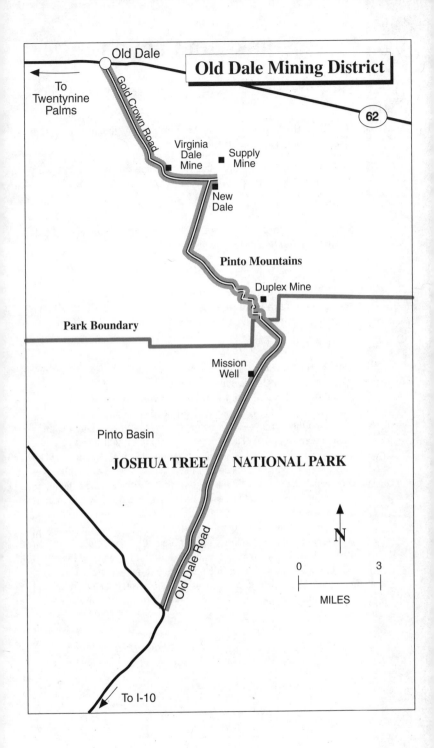

Old Dale

To Twentynine Palms

Old Dale Mining District

62

Gold Crown Road

Virginia Dale Mine

Supply Mine

New Dale

Pinto Mountains

Duplex Mine

Park Boundary

Mission Well

Pinto Basin

JOSHUA TREE   NATIONAL PARK

Old Dale Road

N

0   3

MILES

To I-10

Pinkham Canyon

LOCATION: Joshua Tree National Park, north of I-10. Riverside County.

HIGHLIGHTS: I think you'll be surprised by the relatively lush desert vegetation and beauty along this canyon drive.

DIFFICULTY: Easy to moderate, with sections of soft sand and rocky flood plain. The route can be confusing at times.

TIME & DISTANCE: 2.5 hours; 20 miles.

MAPS: The park's map, ACSC's *Riverside County*, or Trails Illustrated's *Joshua Tree National Park* (No. 226).

INFORMATION: Joshua Tree National Park.

GETTING THERE: The route begins across Cottonwood Spring/Pinto Basin Road from the Cottonwood Spring Visitor Center. You will see the road and a sign. Set your odometer at 0.

REST STOPS: Anywhere you find appealing.

THE DRIVE: This tour starts out as an easy two-track with a few rocky places as it heads into a wash. By mile 8 you will enter the Cottonwood Mountains and Pinkham Canyon, formed at first by low hills and rock cliffs. By mile 12.5 the road is beginning to take you south, and things may seem a bit confusing. You'll be facing toward a hillside here; keep left. There might be a signpost, but in any case you want to continue heading south. By mile 13, well into the rocky canyon, the roadbed will become sandy. You're headed downhill, however, which should make it easier. By mile 18.3 the roadbed should be firm again. Then the road crosses rocky Pinkham Wash, where there is a great deal of ocotillo and a cholla cactus garden (don't touch). Cholla cacti look soft and fuzzy, but they're treacherous. Soon you will see I-10 up ahead, and the Cactus City rest area. You won't be able to exit there, unfortunately, so keep left at about mile 19.1, and soon you will reach a hard-packed dirt service road. Go left, paralleling the freeway, more or less, for several miles. You will come out at a paved road and freeway underpass about 6.5 miles west of Cottonwood Spring Road.

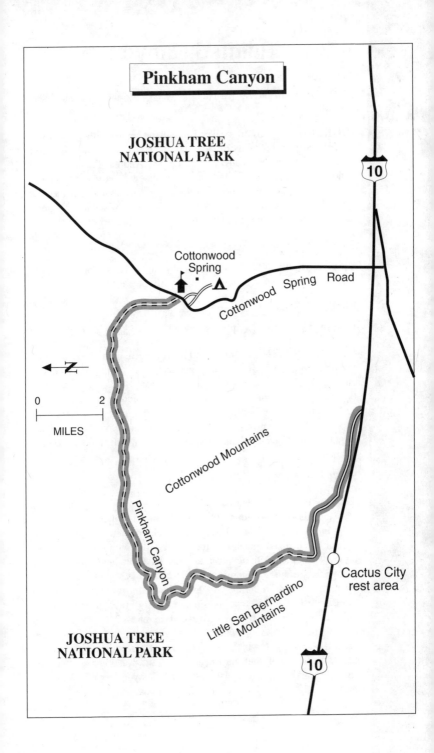

Painted Canyon

LOCATION: In the Mecca Hills, between I-10 and the Salton Sea. Riverside County.

HIGHLIGHTS: This drive takes you into the Mecca Hills Wilderness, a richly colored badlands of steep and jagged sedimentary rock and deeply incised, narrow canyons atop the San Andreas Fault. The road winds through a high-walled canyon with even narrower tributary canyons to explore on foot (one of them, Ladder Canyon, is named for a series of ladders that help hikers scale the steepest sections). I think it's one of the most beautiful desert canyons in California.

DIFFICULTY: Easy 2WD, on a maintained gravel road.

TIME & DISTANCE: 45 minutes to several hours, depending on how much time you spend exploring on foot. About 9.5 miles round-trip.

MAP: ACSC's *Riverside County.*

INFORMATION: BLM Palm Springs-South Coast Field Office.

GETTING THERE: From Hwy. 111 at Mecca: Turn northeast onto Fourth Street, which immediately connects with 66th Ave./Hwy. 195 and bends right (south). In a short distance it bends left (east) to become Box Canyon Road. Continue east through orchards and vineyards and across the Coachella Canal. Then turn left (northwest) at the sign for Painted Canyon Road. **From I-10:** Take Box Canyon Road west toward Mecca for about 15 miles, then turn right (northwest) onto Painted Canyon Road.

REST STOPS: There are many places to stop.

THE DRIVE: Following the graded dirt road, you will soon see the Mecca Hills—steeply up-tilted, layered, folded and incised cliffs of red, pink and gray pastels. The road is a "cherry stem," or legal corridor for mechanized travel, into the Mecca Hills Wilderness. Repeated crustal movements along the San Andreas Fault here have created numerous geologic structures, colorful rock surfaces and vivid patterns. By mile 3 you're in the canyon. Stop along the way and get close to those powerful forces that are simultaneously building and wearing down these mudstone hills. The road ends at mile 4.7. On foot, you can explore the narrows up ahead or the gorgeous, larger high-walled canyon on the right, which ends in a mile at a beautiful dry waterfall basin. Branching off that canyon, on the left side roughly a quarter-mile from the parking area, is the slot of Ladder Canyon. Look for the sign, on your right, that points left to Ladder Canyon.

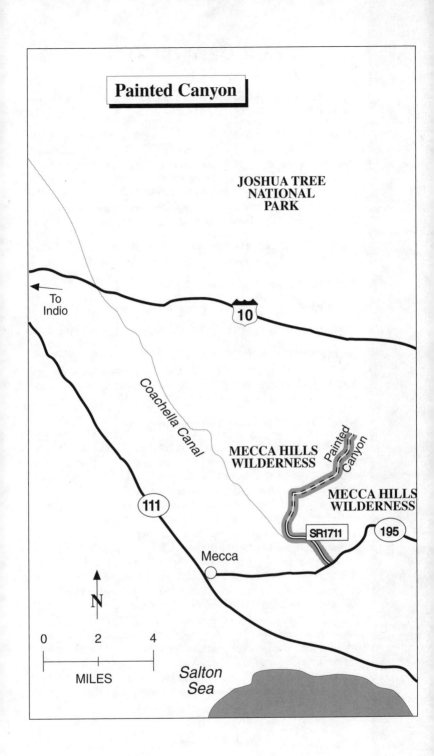

Painted Canyon

JOSHUA TREE
NATIONAL
PARK

To
Indio

10

Coachella Canal

MECCA HILLS
WILDERNESS

Painted Canyon

MECCA HILLS
WILDERNESS

111

SR1711

195

Mecca

N

0   2   4

MILES

Salton
Sea

Red Canyon Trail

LOCATION: In the Orocopia Mountains south of I-10 at Chiriaco Summit. Riverside County.

HIGHLIGHTS: The first few miles follow a "cherry stem," or legal route for mechanized travel, through the Orocopia Mountains Wilderness. The road, which runs along the eastern brink of spectacular Red Canyon, provides sweeping vistas across the Orocopia Mountains to the Chuckwalla and Chocolate mountains. Eventually you will descend into the narrow, high-walled canyon for a unique driving experience. The route ends at historic Bradshaw Trail (Tour 48).

DIFFICULTY: Easy. The first few miles are undulating and serpentine, and may be unpleasant for anyone in the back seat.

TIME & DISTANCE: 1.5 hours; 15.1 miles.

MAP: BLM's *Eagle Mountains* Desert Access Guide.

INFORMATION: BLM's Palm Springs-South Coast Field Office.

GETTING THERE: At Chiriaco Summit, on I-10, follow Pinto Road west along the south side of the interstate for 1.2 miles. Red Canyon Trail (SR2013) begins on the south side of Pinto Road at the information kiosk. Set your odometer to 0.

REST STOPS: You will see some primitive campsites.

THE DRIVE: The road runs south for 1.9 miles, through an off-highway vehicle recreation area, then splits. Keep to the left. From mile 2.4 to mile 8.6 or so, it is flanked by wilderness, so don't venture off the designated route. It's slow going for a time, with small washes, dips, curves and bends, but that will end, and then you will notice a deep, reddish gash in the earth just to the east. That's Red Canyon, and the views into it keep getting better. To the south are the Chocolate Mountains, a military bombing range. To the west are the Orocopia Mountains, home to desert bighorn sheep. To the east is Chuckwalla Bench, home to endangered desert tortoises and one of the best examples in California of a diverse Colorado Desert plant community. There are spurs from the main road that drop into Red Canyon, but I suggest waiting until the posted route at mile 12 to make the descent. Once in the wash, you can drive up-canyon between its high walls for 0.8 mile, where it is blocked by rock. Back at the point where you reached the canyon bottom, continue down-canyon, and in 0.7 mile you will reach Bradshaw Trail. Go left (east) to return to I-10 via Summit Road (taking in Red Cloud Canyon, Tour 45, on the way); or go right (west) on Bradshaw Trail to the Salton Sea.

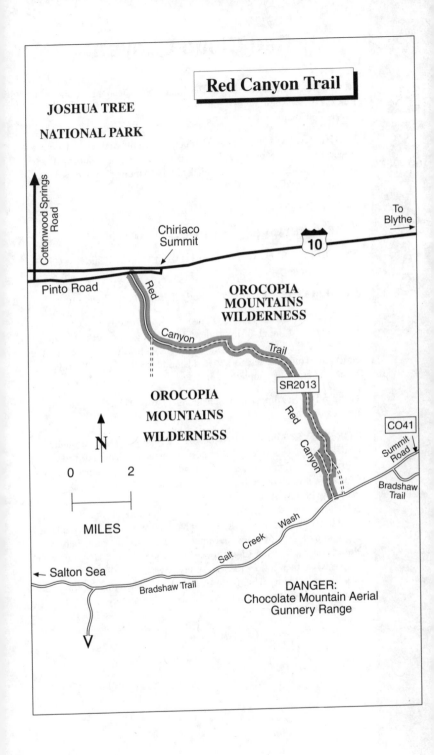

Red Canyon Trail

JOSHUA TREE
NATIONAL PARK

Cottonwood Springs Road

Chiriaco Summit

To Blythe

10

Pinto Road

Red

Canyon

Trail

OROCOPIA
MOUNTAINS
WILDERNESS

SR2013

Red

Canyon

CO41

Summit Road

Bradshaw Trail

OROCOPIA
MOUNTAINS
WILDERNESS

N

0   2

MILES

Salt   Creek   Wash

Salton Sea

Bradshaw Trail

DANGER:
Chocolate Mountain Aerial
Gunnery Range

V

Red Cloud Canyon

LOCATION: South of I-10 in the Chuckwalla Mountains, about 40 miles east of Indio and 9 miles east of I-10's Chiriaco Summit. Riverside County.

HIGHLIGHTS: This is yet another convenient off-highway adventure if you're traveling on I-10. It will take you along a beautiful desert canyon of marbled rock in the Chuckwalla Mountains Wilderness, long a gold-mining district.

DIFFICULTY: Easy, but rocky and bumpy in places.

TIME & DISTANCE: 1.5 hours; 14.6 miles round-trip.

MAPS: BLM's *Eagle Mountains* Desert Access Guide. ACSC's *Riverside County*.

INFORMATION: BLM's Palm Springs-South Coast Field Office.

GETTING THERE: From I-10, take the Red Cloud Road exit. Go 2.1 miles southeast, much of it beside railroad tracks, to a fork. At a junction, the right branch, Summit Road (C041) will take you to the Bradshaw Trail. The left fork is Red Cloud Mine Road, C032. Take the latter, and set your odometer at 0.

REST STOPS: Almost anywhere along the way. There are many primitive campsites.

THE DRIVE: You'll be driving on a designated route through the Chuckwalla Mountains Wilderness, where mechanized travel is restricted to designated roads. This road will take you southeast up Red Cloud Wash to a gorgeous canyon of marbled red and gray rock. It can get pretty bumpy. At mile 2.9, where the road becomes rocky, you will come to a fork; keep right. Do the same at the fork at mile 3.7. Avoid the spurs from the main track; it's not hard to follow. Soon the road will cross a broad area of desert pavement, or flat, broken, varnished rock. Notice the cholla cacti (don't touch!) and ocotillo. Cross a couple of easy washes, then follow the main canyon wash. At mile 7.3 there will be some mine ruins. This is Red Cloud Mine, where, as the old tanks you will see suggest, gold was mined using the cyanide leaching process. Turn around here.

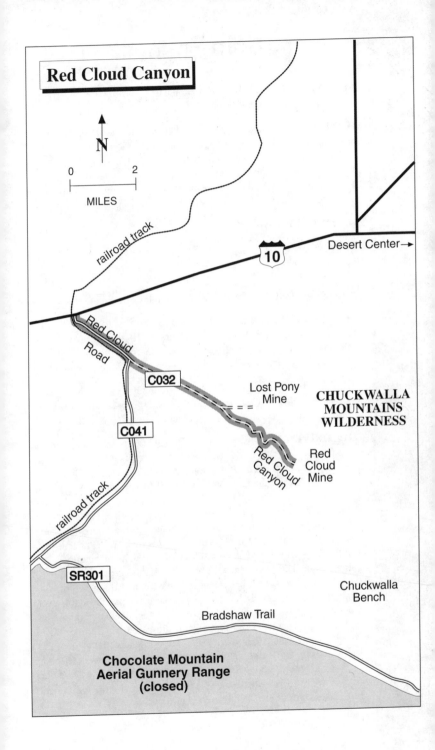

Red Cloud Canyon

Corn Springs

LOCATION: In the Chuckwalla Mountains south of I-10, in southeastern Riverside County.

HIGHLIGHTS: Although the large native California fan palms here have suffered badly from a dropping water table, Corn Springs remains an important oasis surrounded by the Chuckwalla Mountains Wilderness, with rugged desert scenery, abundant vegetation and outstanding panels of Native American petroglyphs, figures of unknown meaning pecked centuries ago into the rock's dark patina.

DIFFICULTY: Easy.

TIME & DISTANCE: 2 hours; 25 miles round-trip.

MAP: ACSC's *Riverside County*.

INFORMATION: BLM Palm Springs-South Coast Field Office.

GETTING THERE: Take I-10 about 9.3 miles east of Desert Center. Take the Corn Springs Road exit; go right (south), then left (southeast) onto Chuckwalla (Chuckwalla Valley on some maps) Road. In half a mile turn right (southwest) onto dirt and gravel Corn Springs Road.

REST STOPS: Corn Springs' fee campground has vault toilets, water, and shade ramadas. There is a half-mile interpretive trail, as well as non-mechanized access to the Chuckwalla Mountains Wilderness.

THE DRIVE: Follow Corn Springs Road (C061) for almost 7 miles from Chuckwalla Road, and suddenly, after you round a bend, you will see of a grove of more than 60 palms, many of them clearly ailing. This area used to have reliable water, but the BLM says drought in recent years has lowered the water table. Corn Springs has supported abundant wildlife, and created an important stopping place for migratory birds. Just before you reach the campground, on the right side of the road, is one of the finest displays of aboriginal rock art in the Colorado Desert. Rock art is found on both sides of the wash in the vicinity of the campground. The earliest may be as old as 10,000 years, according to the BLM, but most of it is thought to be less than 1,000 years old. To continue the drive, veer left at the campground, past a nature trail. Continue west on the dirt-and-gravel road for about 3 miles. Now you're driving across desert pavement, following Corn Springs Wash. At Aztec Well, where there are a handful of residences, the road for this tour angles up to the right. Notice how lush and diverse the desert vegetation is. It includes ocotillo, cholla and barrel cacti. About 2.5 miles from Aztec Well you will come to a flat and open spot at the base of a hill. Take a break here, then retrace your route.

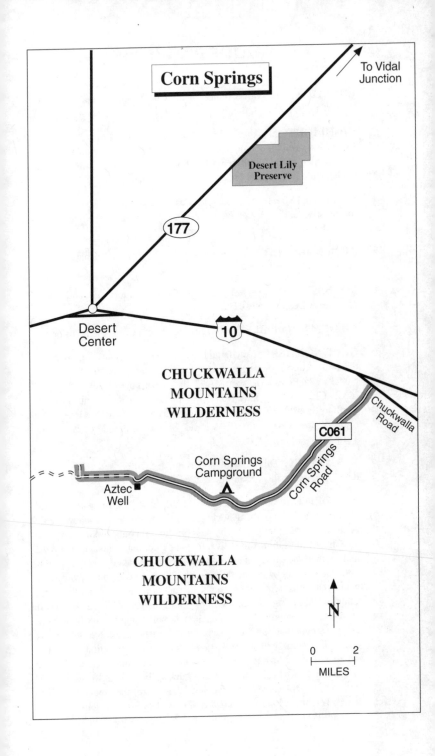

Augustine Pass

LOCATION: Riverside County, in the Chuckwalla Mountains south of I-10 and west of Blythe.

HIGHLIGHTS: This tour starts at the historic Bradshaw Trail (Tour 48), crosses remote Augustine Pass (about 2,300 feet), then follows a narrow, serpentine and beautiful high-walled canyon through the Chuckwalla Mountains, once a gold-mining district.

DIFFICULTY: Easy to moderate. Less experienced drivers may find the twisting and rocky canyon segment difficult. The roads are well-marked with BLM signposts.

TIME & DISTANCE: 1.5 hours; 15.8 miles from Bradshaw Trail to Graham Pass Road.

MAPS: ACSC's *Riverside County*. BLM's *Salton Sea* and *Eagle Mountains* Desert Access Guides.

INFORMATION: BLM's Palm Springs-South Coast Field Office.

GETTING THERE: You can drive either north or south, approaching the route from any of several directions. I suggest taking I-10 to the Chuckwalla Road exit, west of Blythe. Then take Chuckwalla Road (a.k.a. Chuckwalla Valley Road) to Graham Pass Road, and follow it south to Bradshaw Trail. Go west on Bradshaw Trail for 8.8 miles. The route begins at Augustine Pass Road, on the north side of Bradshaw Trail.

REST STOPS: This is wild and rugged country, and there are no developed campsites or facilities of any kind.

THE DRIVE: From the Bradshaw Trail, little Augustine Pass Road climbs steadily into the Chuckwalla Mountains and reaches scenic Augustine Pass at mile 1.9. The pass provides an outstanding view into the Chuckwallas, home to a diverse range of desert plants and animals, and south to the Chocolate Mountains. From the pass the road descends into a narrow, rocky ravine that soon becomes a deep and narrow rock-walled canyon. By mile 4.6 you will reach a posted road on the right, Chuckwalla Springs Road. It climbs out of the canyon via a short shelf segment, and emerges onto a bench. You will connect with it later on. For now, continue down the wash for 2.4 miles. The route, which has been going north, will suddenly bend right (southeast), climb out of the wash and head toward the mountains again. In a short distance Augustine Pass Road will come to Chuckwalla Springs Road. Go left, and follow it basically northeast along the base of the mountains. Soon it will become a long straightaway that will eventually deliver you to Graham Pass Road. Go left (north) to Chuckwalla Road and I-10.

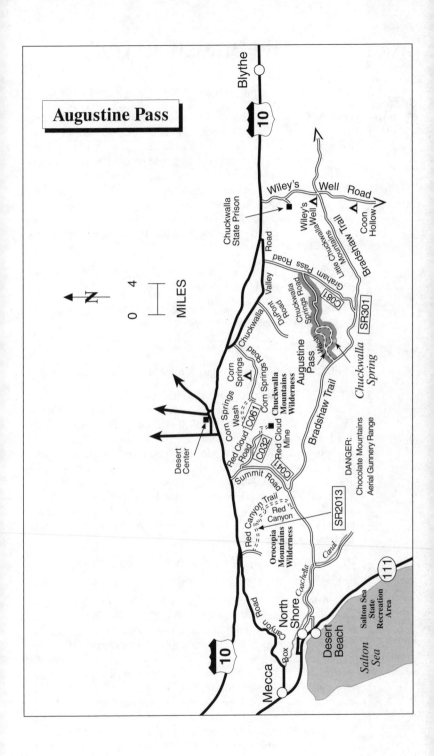

Augustine Pass

The Bradshaw Trail

LOCATION: East of the Salton Sea. South of I-10. Riverside County.

HIGHLIGHTS: William Bradshaw established the first road across Riverside County in 1862, linking San Bernardino with the Colorado River and the gold mines at La Paz (now Ehrenberg), Arizona. Its use virtually ended by 1877, due to falling gold production and construction of the railroad to Yuma, Arizona. Today, it provides views of the Orocopia and Chuckwalla mountains. It crosses the sloping Chuckwalla Bench, noted for a diverse Colorado Desert plant community that includes the rare 6- to 15-foot-tall Munz cholla cactus. The bench is also home to bighorn sheep, raptors, the endangered desert tortoise, and many other animals.

DIFFICULTY: Easy, but with stretches of soft sand at the east end. Avoid the military's live bombing range.

TIME & DISTANCE: 4 hours; 77 miles. It can be taken in segments via Graham Pass and Summit roads.

MAP: ACSC's *Riverside County*.

INFORMATION: BLM's Palms Springs-South Coast Field Office.

GETTING THERE: To go west, the direction I prefer for vistas of the Salton Sea and the Santa Rosa Mountains**:** From I-10 about 17 miles west of Blythe, take the Wiley's Well exit. Go south on Wiley's Well Road. The pavement ends at the turnoff to Chuckwalla State Prison. Continue south on the unpaved road. 8.6 miles south of I-10 is the junction with the Bradshaw Trail (SR301). Go right (west). **To go east:** Take Hwy. 111 to Salton Sea State Recreation Area. Across the highway from park headquarters is Parkside Drive. Go east on Parkside Drive for 1.7 miles, then go left (north) onto Desert Aire. Drive a half-mile to Coachella Canal. Take the canal road east for about 10 miles to the Drop 24 facility and turn left.

REST STOPS: At the east end are Wiley's Well and Coon Hollow campgrounds, which lack potable water.

THE DRIVE: Just north of the meandering Bradshaw Trail, which varies from rudimentary desert trail to graded gravel and sand, loom two rugged and beautiful mountain ranges, the Orocopia and the Chuckwalla. Both are largely designated wilderness areas where, but for the occasional "cherry stem," mechanized travel is not allowed. In between is the Chuckwalla Bench. South of the road is the Chocolate Mountain Aerial Gunnery Range. Along the way are craggy cliffs, deep canyons, bajadas (raised plains of merging alluvial fans), sandy washes and expanses of desert pavement. There are nine species of cacti as well as ocotillo and creosote bush. In fact, the array of life here demonstrates that ostensibly barren deserts are anything but.

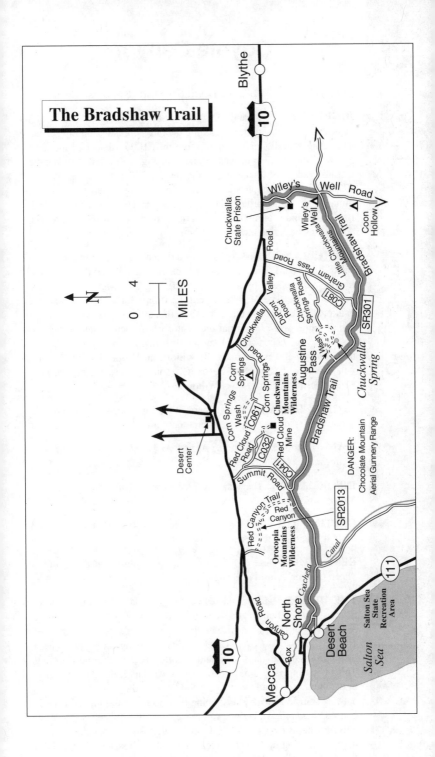

The Bradshaw Trail

127

Coyote Canyon

LOCATION: Anza-Borrego Desert State Park. San Diego County.

HIGHLIGHTS: The canyon's wetlands and year-round creek sustain an array of desert wildlife, including the rare Peninsular bighorn sheep and the least Bells vireo, one of more than 100 bird species that nest and feed in the canyon. Hiking and camping are available in remote Collins Valley. Scan the high hillsides for isolated palm groves. In 1775, 240 colonists from Mexico, led by Juan Bautista de Anza, brought 800 cattle through the canyon, where they camped during the first overland colonizing expedition to Alta California. Native Americans occupied the area for thousands of years before that.

DIFFICULTY: It's easy as far as, and then beyond, a 0.6-mile section called the bypass road—a difficult, rock-strewn 4x4 trail that begins at Lower Willows and bypasses Coyote Creek. That segment is not for novices. Some type of vehicle damage, if only undercarriage scrapes, is likely. There are also three crossings of Coyote Creek. The third one can be quite deep; inquire at the visitor center before setting out. To assure bighorn sheep access to water, the canyon is permanently closed to motor vehicles between Middle Willows and Upper Willows, so you will have to backtrack. The entire route is closed June through September just before Lower Willows.

TIME & DISTANCE: 4-5 hours; 11.8 miles one-way to Middle Willows. Exploring will add several more miles.

MAPS: The park's brochure. *Anza-Borrego Desert State Park and adjacent areas* (Wilderness Press).

INFORMATION: The visitor center is open daily October through May, 9 a.m.-5 p.m.

GETTING THERE: From Borrego Springs, take Di Giorgio Road north 4.6 miles to the former fee-collection station.

REST STOPS: Desert Gardens has picnic tables. You can camp at Sheep Canyon Primitive Camp.

THE DRIVE: The road passes ocotillo, cholla cactus and creosote bush as you head up what appears more like a valley than a canyon. At mile 3 is Desert Gardens, with its array of desert plants. At 3.4 the road crosses the wash of Coyote Creek, at First Crossing. At 4.7 you enter a lush portion of Coyote Creek, and ford the creek at Second Crossing. Third Crossing is at 5.5, at Lower Willows. Here, decide whether to brave the bypass road, which goes to Collins Valley. If you do, at mile 6.4 is a spur to a marker describing the Anza expedition, and a viewpoint. Once in the valley you can make a circuit to Sheep, Cougar and Salvador canyons. Continuing to the road closure at Middle Willows involves driving up Coyote Creek's rocky bed. It's slow going, and is worthwhile only if you want to hike farther up Coyote Canyon.

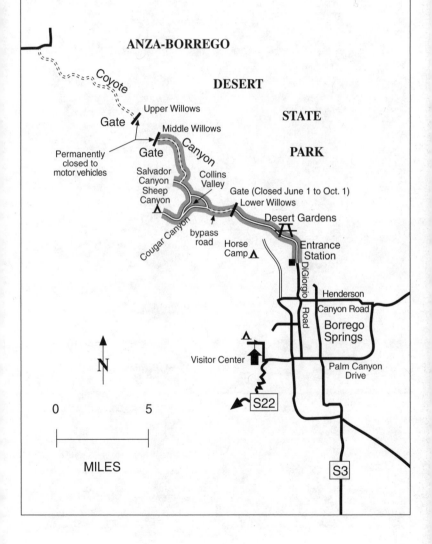

Coyote Canyon

ANZA-BORREGO

DESERT

STATE

PARK

Coyote

Canyon

Upper Willows

Gate

Middle Willows

Permanently
closed to
motor vehicles

Gate

Salvador
Canyon
Sheep
Canyon

Collins
Valley

Gate (Closed June 1 to Oct. 1)

Lower Willows

Desert Gardens

Cougar Canyon

bypass
road

Horse
Camp

Entrance
Station

DiGiorgio Road

Henderson

Canyon Road

Borrego
Springs

Visitor Center

Palm Canyon
Drive

S22

N

0   5

MILES

S3

Desert bighorn, Coyote Canyon *(Tour 49)*

Borrego Badlands from Font's Point *(Tour 50)*

Font's Point

LOCATION: Anza-Borrego Desert State Park. San Diego County.

HIGHLIGHTS: This sandy desert wash route is a short and convenient opportunity to sample the park's network of rudimentary backways. It ends at a clifftop point with a spectacular view across a vast, forbidding expanse of the Colorado Desert. If you've never driven in a desert wash, this route provides an ideal introductory experience.

DIFFICULTY: Easy, but very sandy. Inquire at the visitor center for current conditions. Follow the tracks of the established roadway.

TIME & DISTANCE: 1 hour; 7.8 miles round-trip.

MAP: The park's map is very good.

INFORMATION: Anza-Borrego Desert State Park.

GETTING THERE: The turnoff is 3.7 miles east of where paved road S22 (the Borrego-Salton Seaway) makes a sharp bend to the east; or 8.8 miles from the intersection of Borrego Valley Road and Palm Canyon Drive. Turn south at the sign.

REST STOPS: You won't need one on this short drive.

THE DRIVE: Drive directly up wide Font's Wash (Font's Point Wash on some maps) to Font's Point, where the view extends across the Borrego Badlands to the Salton Sea, Borrego Buttes, meandering San Felipe Wash and the Fish Creek Mountains. The colorful sediments that you will gaze upon range in age from 250,000 years to 2 million years. The fossil record shows that this region once was a landscape of streams and meadows, and was home to freshwater snails, clams, ice-age horses, camels, sloths, bears and mammoths. The point also overlooks the historic Anza Trail, traveled by California's first overland immigrants in 1775. The point is named for Father Pedro Font, chaplain and diarist during Spanish explorer Juan Bautista de Anza's second journey through this forbidding place in 1775-1776, when he led 240 settlers and soldiers and 800 head of cattle from Mexico to San Francisco Bay.

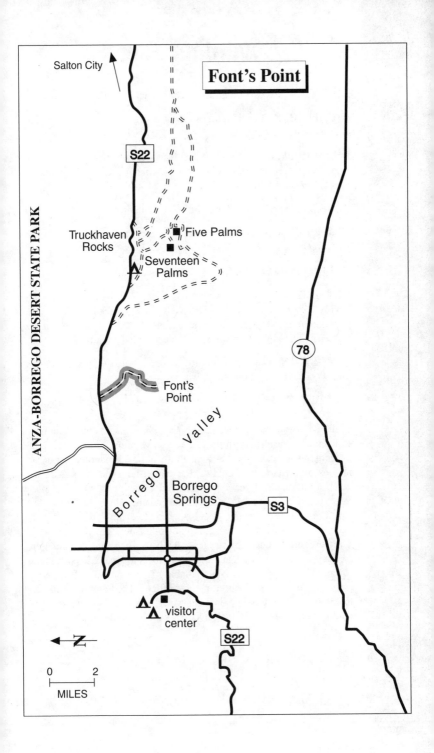

Font's Point

Salton City

S22

ANZA-BORREGO DESERT STATE PARK

Truckhaven
Rocks

Five Palms

Seventeen
Palms

78

Font's
Point

Valley

Borrego

Borrego
Springs

S3

visitor
center

S22

N

0   2
MILES

Seventeen Palms

LOCATION: Anza-Borrego Desert State Park. San Diego County.

HIGHLIGHTS: This is quite a fun, if short, desert wash drive that ends at a historic palm oasis.

DIFFICULTY: Easy to moderate. Soft sand may be a problem in a few places, and there are some rocky stretches. Inquire at the visitor center for current conditions.

TIME & DISTANCE: 1 hour; 7.6 miles round-trip.

MAPS: The park's map is adequate. *Anza-Borrego Desert Region State Park and adjacent areas* (Wilderness Press) is useful as well.

INFORMATION: Anza-Borrego Desert State Park.

GETTING THERE: From Christmas Circle in Borrego Springs, take road S22 east for 15.7 miles. Turn right (southeast) into a wash. Set your odometer to 0. You may see a sign stating "Arroyo Salado" on the right, and a nearby signpost for the Seventeen Palms trail.

REST STOPS: There is a primitive camping area with vault toilets (but no tables) early along the drive.

THE DRIVE: Drive down Arroyo Salado, passing the camping area, for about 3.8 miles, then veer right. In a short distance you will come to the parking area for the oasis, where there is a stone monument explaining its historic significance. The grove of native palms is nearby, looking just like the oases in those old French Foreign Legion movies. You will be the latest in a stream of visitors who've been drawn here for thousands of years. Nomadic Indians, emigrants and prospectors have all come to this island in the badlands for water, shade and rest. The oasis is a remnant of an era when grasslands, streams, camels and mammoths shared a very different world from what you see today. The palms are sustained by surface water here. The spring is unreliable, so early travelers would leave water for others in large glass jars in the shade. (The spring's water is not potable.) They would also leave written messages in the "prospector's post office." The tradition continues today; check the middle palms for water jugs and daily diaries, and you'll see that people from all over the world come here.

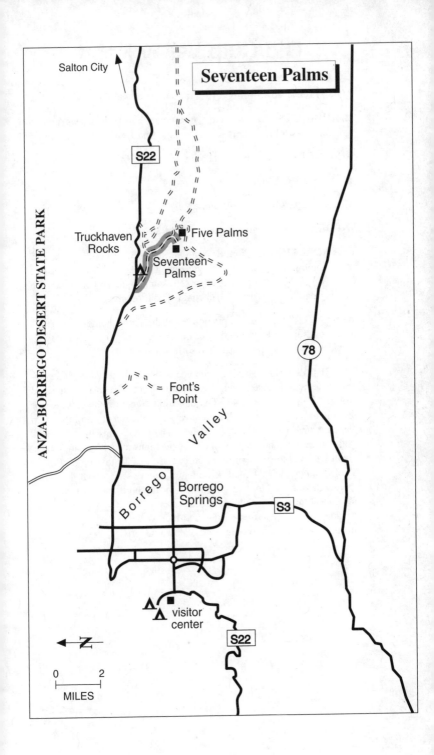

Seventeen Palms

Salton City

S22

Truckhaven Rocks

Five Palms

Seventeen Palms

ANZA-BORREGO DESERT STATE PARK

78

Font's Point

Valley

Borrego

Borrego Springs

S3

visitor center

S22

N

0   2
MILES

Old Culp Valley Road

LOCATION: Anza-Borrego Desert State Park. San Diego County.

HIGHLIGHTS: This is a short, convenient and pretty drive through mountains with lush desert vegetation and fine views.

DIFFICULTY: Easy, but there are a few rough spots.

TIME & DISTANCE: 1 hour; 5.5 miles.

MAP: The park's map is adequate.

INFORMATION: Anza-Borrego Desert State Park.

GETTING THERE: From Borrego Springs, take road S22 about 11.5 miles southwest, up the steep Montezuma Grade. The route begins 0.4 mile west of the park entrance. Turn left (south) onto the two-track road running parallel to Wilson Road, and set your odometer at 0.

REST STOPS: There is a picnic area at the Paroli homesite. There's also the Culp Valley Primitive Camp Area. Borrego Springs has all services, and some very upscale resorts.

THE DRIVE: At the starting point you will be at almost 4,000 feet elevation, amid a diverse range of vegetation. Yet to the east lies the arid Borrego Valley, at about 450 feet elevation. Such are the contrasts of this rugged region. You will have a very pretty descent into little Culp Valley, which lies at about 2,800 feet. The tour begins by crossing a grassy meadow. Then, at 0.6 mile from the highway, take a hard left. In about half a mile you will reach an intersection. To the right is Jasper Trail, a moderate 4x4 road. Continue straight. After about 4.9 miles there will be a road to the right, which goes a short distance to the picnic area at the old Paroli homesite. Soon the road enters a meadow surrounded by boulder-strewn hills, and then you will reach paved S22. Borrego Springs is to the right, back down the grade.

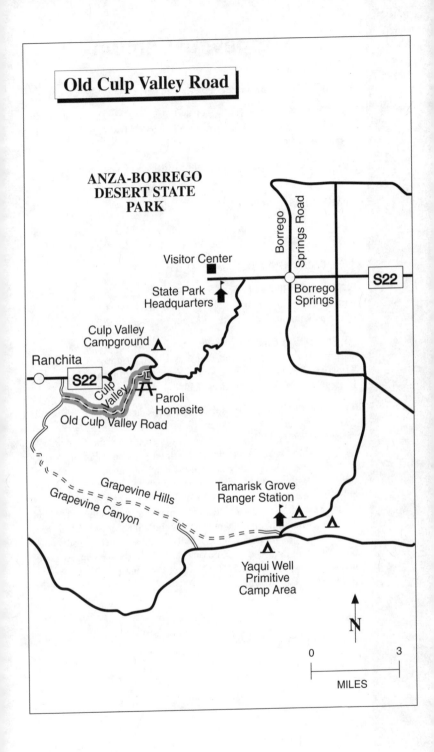

Old Culp Valley Road

ANZA-BORREGO DESERT STATE PARK

Visitor Center

State Park Headquarters

Borrego Springs Road

Borrego Springs

S22

Culp Valley Campground

Ranchita

S22

Culp Valley

Paroli Homesite

Old Culp Valley Road

Grapevine Hills

Grapevine Canyon

Tamarisk Grove Ranger Station

Yaqui Well Primitive Camp Area

N

0   3

MILES

Grapevine Canyon

LOCATION: Anza-Borrego Desert State Park. San Diego County.

HIGHLIGHTS: This little road provides fine views and changing desert vegetation as it takes you from almost 4,000 feet elevation to about 1,400 feet.

DIFFICULTY: Easy, with a few short stretches of sand and rough road surface.

TIME & DISTANCE: 1.5 hours; 13 miles.

MAPS: The park's map. ACSC's *San Diego County. Anza-Borrego Desert Region State Park and adjacent areas* (Wilderness Press).

INFORMATION: Anza-Borrego Desert State Park.

GETTING THERE: From Borrego Springs, take road S22 southwest up the steep grade for about 11.5 miles. Turn left (south) 0.4 mile west of the park entrance onto Wilson Road. Set your odometer at 0 here.

REST STOPS: Culp Valley Primitive Camp Area on the way to the starting point. Or at the end, the Yaqui Well Primitive Camp Area, Tamarisk Grove Campground, or the Yaqui Pass Primitive Camp Area. Borrego Springs has all services, including some upscale resorts.

THE DRIVE: You'll pass some private residences on this drive, so take it slow and be considerate. After about 2.7 miles, when you descend into Grapevine Canyon, you will come to a T intersection. Go left (southeast). Signs along the way will let you know that the people who live here take privacy and safe driving seriously. After about 4 miles you will pass Grapevine Springs Ranch and Vineyards, and then cross into the park, following some power lines. There will be a short stretch of sand. At mile 4.7 watch for wild grapevines on the left. About 1.3 miles from that point, there's a tricky little intersection. Look for a post, and go around it and to the left. The road will be more adventurous from here as you descend along the side of the canyon. At about mile 8.7 is a right turn to Hwy. 78, but continue past Yaqui Well to paved Yaqui Pass Road (S3).

Grapevine Canyon

Anza-Borrego
Desert State Park

Visitor Center

State Park
Headquarters

Culp Valley
Campground

Ranchita

S22

Culp Valley

Paroli
Homesite

Old Culp Valley Road

Grapevine Hills

Grapevine Canyon

Tamarisk Grove
Ranger Station

Borrego Springs Road

S22

Borrego
Springs

N

0   3

MILES

Fish Creek Wash

LOCATION: Anza-Borrego Desert State Park. San Diego County.

HIGHLIGHTS: If you do only one drive in the park, do this one. It has it all: an outstanding scenic and geologic experience, wind caves, a primeval landscape, and Sandstone Canyon, a long slot canyon with walls some 200 feet high.

DIFFICULTY: Easy to moderate. You may encounter soft sand and fallen rock. Check with the visitor center for current conditions.

TIME & DISTANCE: 4 hours; almost 25 miles.

MAPS: The park's map. *Anza-Borrego Desert Region State Park and adjacent areas* (Wilderness Press).

INFORMATION: Anza-Borrego Desert State Park.

GETTING THERE: Take Hwy. 78 to Ocotillo Wells. Go south on Split Mountain Road. At mile 7.9 you'll reach Fish Creek Wash. Set your odometer at 0. Go right (west) up the wash.

REST STOPS: Fish Creek Primitive Campground, early on the drive, has toilets and tables, but no water. Dispersed camping is allowed, but fires must be in metal containers. You must use your own wood and haul out the ashes.

THE DRIVE: Head up wide, gravely Fish Creek Wash toward the split in Split Mountain, which was created by powerful floods cutting through rising mountains. The action has exposed colorful red walls, cobbles and, at mile 3.6, fascinating pressure bends, or anticlines, in the canyon's rock strata, which you will see on your right. The split separates the Vallecito Mountains on the right (west) and Fish Creek Mountains on the left (east). At mile 4.2, on the left, is the trailhead for the 20-minute hike up to the wind caves, huge rocks honeycombed with holes and caves. The view from them takes in Elephant Knees (a fossilized reef of compacted oyster beds), and the Carrizo Badlands. Drive along the base of sandstone cliffs, and at mile 6.8 you will see the Loop Wash spur, on the right. (It's similar to Fish Creek Wash but narrower, with sandy spots and possible rockfalls. It rejoins Fish Creek Wash 2 miles farther ahead.) At about mile 12.4 look left for the sign for Sandstone Canyon, a high-walled slot in the rock cliffs. It's driveable, technically, but it becomes very narrow (you will see paint on the rocks from vehicles that have squeezed through). You may also find it blocked by rocks and boulders. I suggest walking into it. Afterwards, retrace your route to return to Split Mountain Road.

Fish Creek Wash

Borrego Springs Road

78

Ocotillo Wells

Lower Borrego Valley

Split Mountain Road

ANZA-BORREGO DESERT STATE PARK

Elephant Tree Area

Fish Creek Wash

Vallecito Mountains

Split Mountain

Sandstone Canyon

Loop Wash

Wind Caves

Fish Creek Mountains

Carrizo Badlands

Diablo Dropoff

N

0   3
MILES

Fossil Canyon

LOCATION: North of Ocotillo, off I-8 in the Coyote Mountains Wilderness. Imperial County.

HIGHLIGHTS: This is another colorful, narrow desert canyon, and another opportunity to break up a long freeway trek with a short and convenient side trip. You will explore a fascinating canyon known for the abundant marine fossils in its walls and its 7- to 20-million-year geologic history. Once largely driveable, much of the canyon is now restricted to foot traffic, which for many visitors will make the experience even better.

DIFFICULTY: Easy.

TIME & DISTANCE: 1.5 hours; about 3.5 miles. A gate in the canyon marks the wilderness boundary, beyond which mechanized travel is not permitted. Hike from there.

MAPS: ACSC's *Imperial County. Anza-Borrego Desert Region State Park and adjacent areas* (Wilderness Press). BLM's *El Cajon* Desert Access Guide.

INFORMATION: BLM's El Centro Field Office.

GETTING THERE: From I-8, take the Ocotillo/Imperial Highway (Hwy. S2) exit. Follow S2 through Ocotillo. At a stop sign shortly after the sharp bend to the left, go right (north) onto Shell Canyon Road. The pavement will end. The turnoff to Fossil Canyon is 0.15 mile after you pass beneath the power lines, as the main road makes a long westward bend. If you reach the gravel operation, you've missed it.

REST STOPS: Anywhere you find appealing. El Centro has all services.

THE DRIVE: This sandstone canyon, like Painted Gorge (Tour 56), cuts through a thick layer of sediment in an area that at different times in the Earth's past lay beneath an inland sea and a large lake. The reddish-yellow layers of sedimentary rock were laid down over the eons, and then were rearranged by geologic forces. You won't get too far up the canyon before you encounter a wide section where you can park, an information kiosk and a gate.

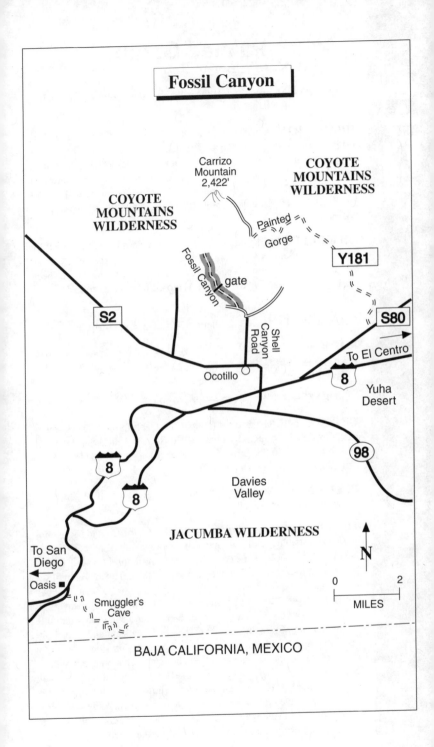

Fossil Canyon

COYOTE
MOUNTAINS
WILDERNESS

Carrizo
Mountain
2,422'

COYOTE
MOUNTAINS
WILDERNESS

Painted
Gorge

Y181

Fossil Canyon

gate

S2

Shell
Canyon
Road

S80

To El Centro

8

Ocotillo

Yuha
Desert

98

Davies
Valley

8

8

JACUMBA WILDERNESS

N

To San
Diego

Oasis

Smuggler's
Cave

0   2
MILES

BAJA CALIFORNIA, MEXICO

Painted Gorge

LOCATION: Northeast of Ocotillo, in the Coyote Mountains. Imperial County.

HIGHLIGHTS: Painted Gorge, as the name suggests, is a narrow, colorful cleft of sedimentary rock. The many hues stem from the rock's copper, sulfur and iron content. The upper gorge contains fossilized coral reefs and marine life, as well as "shell hash," a mix of crushed ancient shells that often goes unnoticed by folks who are actually walking on it. This is an outstanding side trip to break up a long freeway journey.

DIFFICULTY: Moderate. There is one very narrow spot to carefully creep through, and some rocky stretches. **Note:** To protect the Coyote Mountains' population of endangered Peninsular Ranges bighorn sheep during lambing season, the canyon is closed to vehicles from Jan. 1 to June 30.

TIME & DISTANCE: 1.5-2 hours; 14.5 miles round-trip.

MAPS: *Anza-Borrego Desert Region State Park and adjacent areas* (Wilderness Press). BLM's *El Centro* Desert Access Guide. ACSC's *Imperial County.*

INFORMATION: BLM's El Centro Field Office.

GETTING THERE: From I-8, take the Ocotillo/Imperial Highway exit. Go east on Imperial County Road S80, and in about 4.2 miles you'll see a sign for the turnoff (left, or north) onto Painted Gorge Road (Y181). Set your odometer at 0.

REST STOPS: There are primitive camping sites east of the gorge entrance. El Centro has all services.

THE DRIVE: Painted Gorge is surrounded by the Coyote Mountains Wilderness. Oddly, not far to the north are a number of military bombing ranges, but such are the competing interests in the California desert. Anyway, at the outset look south, and about 100 feet away you will see the tracks of the old Arizona & Eastern San Diego Railroad, dubbed "the impossible railroad" because of the difficult terrain it traversed. After mile 1.4 you will pass some residences and enter the seemingly barren Coyote Mountains. At about mile 3.5 is a sand and gravel pit; drive through it, and you'll find the road on the other side. Keep right at the Y at mile 4.4. At mile 4.7 is yet another Y. That branch will peter out in a short distance, so keep right. After another 0.2 mile you will reach yet another Y, in a little bowl of yellow rock. Go left, between two bushes, drive up a wash and enter a very narrow gorge of colored rocks. You will eventually reach a point where the road makes a hard right, and climbs as a rough 4x4 trail. Turn around here.

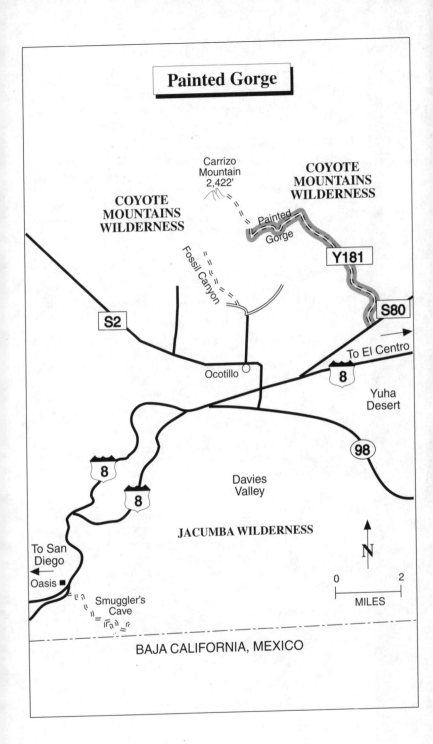

Painted Gorge

Carrizo Mountain 2,422'

COYOTE MOUNTAINS WILDERNESS

COYOTE MOUNTAINS WILDERNESS

Painted Gorge

Fossil Canyon

Y181

S80

S2

To El Centro

8

Ocotillo

Yuha Desert

98

Davies Valley

8

8

JACUMBA WILDERNESS

N

0 2

MILES

To San Diego

Oasis ■

Smuggler's Cave

BAJA CALIFORNIA, MEXICO

Elliott Mine Area

LOCATION: 85 miles east of San Diego, in Imperial County just east of the San Diego County-Imperial County line and immediately south of I-8.

HIGHLIGHTS: This route through a strange jumble of granite rocks and boulders is up against the boundary of the Jacumba Wilderness, and goes to within a quarter-mile or so of the Mexican border. The rocks have formed piles and towers that create mazes and caves, and provide excellent views. East of the road, in the wilderness area, is Smuggler's Cave, a hollow said to have been used by smugglers and bandits in the late 1800s and early 1900s.

DIFFICULTY: Moderate as far as I take you.

TIME & DISTANCE: 1-1.5 hours; about 4.5 miles round-trip.

MAPS: BLM's *El Cajon* Desert Access Guide. ACSC's *San Diego County*.

INFORMATION: BLM's El Centro Field Office.

GETTING THERE: From eastbound I-8 near the San Diego County-Imperial County line, take the In-Ko-Pah Park Road exit. Go right at the bottom of the exit, then right again on paved Old Hwy. 80, and go almost 0.2 mile. Turn left onto a dirt area, then immediately left again and you're on the route, Y2219.

REST STOPS: There are outstanding places to hike into in the Jacumba Wilderness, including another jumble of massive granite boulders, Valley of the Moon.

THE DRIVE: Follow the single-lane road up a steep hill, the steepest parts of which have been crudely paved. Keep left when you reach a fork. The right fork is very bad, and reconnects to the main route anyway in a short distance. You will have some great views as you climb to about 3,700 feet. Before descending toward the rocks, check the road ahead to be sure that no one is coming up in the opposite direction. If someone is, yield, since uphill traffic has the right of way. On the way down you may encounter a particularly nasty, but short, bit of roadbed. Use low range, and take it slow. Not too much farther things will get too rough to continue, at least in my opinion, so find a good place to stop and explore the area on foot. The road ends at the old, inactive Elliott amethyst mine.

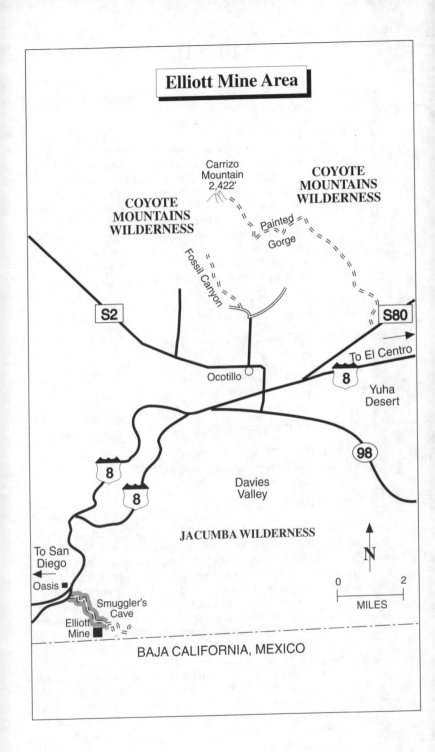

Elliott Mine Area

COYOTE MOUNTAINS WILDERNESS

Carrizo Mountain 2,422'

COYOTE MOUNTAINS WILDERNESS

Painted Gorge

Fossil Canyon

S2

S80

To El Centro

8

Yuha Desert

Ocotillo

8

8

98

Davies Valley

JACUMBA WILDERNESS

N

To San Diego

Oasis

Smuggler's Cave

Elliott Mine

0 2 MILES

BAJA CALIFORNIA, MEXICO

Yuha Basin

LOCATION: About 25 miles east of Calexico between I-8 and Hwy. 98. Imperial County.

HIGHLIGHTS: There is a maze of roads through the fascinating hills, badlands, flats and washes of the Yuha Basin. The BLM does try to keep them posted, but signposts don't last long in the wild, so don't be surprised or disappointed if you end up doing quite a bit of exploring in this historic area. Yuha Well is where Capt. Juan Bautista de Anza, the Spanish explorer who established the first overland emigrant trail from Mexico to San Francisco Bay, camped during two expeditions in the 1770s. The oyster-shell fossil beds here are left over from an ancient sea that covered most of Imperial and central Riverside counties five to six million years ago. The Yuha Geoglyphs are prehistoric ground symbols attributed to the Kamia people.

DIFFICULTY: Easy to moderate, depending on whether you encounter sand. It can be a confusing place.

TIME & DISTANCE: 1.5-2 hours; 14 miles, depending on how much route-finding and exploring you do.

MAPS: ACSC's *Imperial County. Anza-Borrego Desert Region State Park and adjacent areas* (Wilderness Press). BLM's *El Centro* Desert Access Guide.

INFORMATION: BLM's El Centro Field Office.

GETTING THERE: Exit I-8 at Ocotillo. Take Imperial County Road S2 right (south) a short distance to Hwy. 98. Go left (east) for 5.9 miles. Turn left (north) onto dirt road Y1928.

REST STOPS: Primitive camping is allowed.

THE DRIVE: From the highway, take Y1928 for 0.8 mile to a Y. Go straight, staying on Y1928. It will curve northeast along the western rim of the basin, past the fenced Yuha Geoglyphs, which vandals nearly destroyed in 1975. The designs were reconstructed in 1981, but they've been vandalized again. Made by scraping away the desert pavement to reveal the lighter sand below, it is thought that they were used in rituals commemorating myths, and for purification dances. About 4 miles from that first Y, a road to the right (southwest), Y1950, will take you in a bit more than a mile to the Yuha Well area, where the de Anza expeditions camped. Led by Indian guides, de Anza established an overland trail between today's Tubac, Arizona (Sonora, Mexico, back then) and the Pacific Coast. Farther on, road Y1945 goes to the oyster-shell fossil beds. Dense beds of fossilized shells are found here. The main route, now Y1950, continues northeast another 3.5 miles or so to I-8 and Dunaway Road. Note: To visit the overlook and the monument to the explorer that is noted on the map, go right at that first Y, onto road Y2739, and drive 0.8 mile.

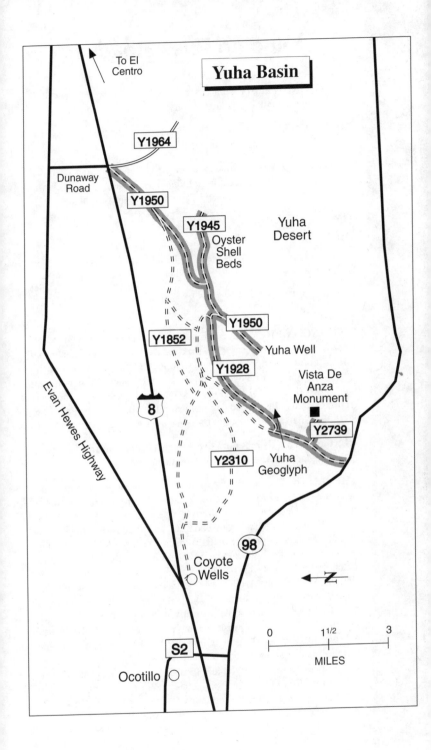

Indian Pass Road

LOCATION: North of Yuma, Arizona, just west of Picacho State Recreation Area in the Chocolate Mountains. Imperial County.

HIGHLIGHTS: The Colorado Desert scenery here along the Colorado River is stark, forbidding and beautiful.

DIFFICULTY: Easy to moderate. There is a narrow, rocky, eroded stretch of road on the descent from Indian Pass to sandy Gavilan Wash. The segment along the river can be flooded in periods of high water.

TIME & DISTANCE: 2.5 hours; 23 miles from Ogilby Road to Picacho.

MAPS: ACSC's *Imperial County*. BLM's *Yuma* and *Trigo Mountains* Desert Access Guides.

INFORMATION: Picacho State Recreation Area. BLM's El Centro Field Office.

GETTING THERE: This drive can be taken in either direction, but since it involves sandy stretches I recommend the downhill direction. So I describe it going west to east, starting at Ogilby Road. **From the south:** Take I-8 east beyond Imperial Sand Dunes. Turn north on Ogilby Road (Imperial Co. Road S34), and go 13.1 miles. Turn east (right) on Indian Pass Road (A272). **From the north:** Take Hwy. 78 to S34; take S34 south 10.4 miles to Indian Pass Road.

REST STOPS: There's primitive camping along Indian Pass Road, and developed fee sites in the recreation area.

THE DRIVE: The graded dirt road crosses a broad, open region and heads toward a tall rock fin on the horizon, passing stands of ocotillo, cholla cactus and creosote bush. You'll pass numerous sandy washes lined with palo verde and ironwood trees, and after a wet winter spring wildflowers can be profuse. After 6 miles you'll see the road heading toward a gap in the hills, and jagged peaks beyond the gap. The gap is Indian Pass. At 1,040 feet above sea level, it is your entrance to a corridor flanked by the Indian Pass Wilderness to the north, and the Picacho Peak Wilderness to the south. Beyond the pass lies the half-mile descent along Gavilan Wash, a narrow, rocky and eroded track. Go right when you reach the wash, staying on the main tracks for the next 6.2 miles, to a fork. A sign may indicate that 4-S Ranch, a boat ramp and primitive camping area, are left. You can go that way and explore, but the main route goes right, and for the next 7.6 miles you will have a beautiful drive along the Colorado River to the site of Picacho, a gold-mining town a century ago, and today a state park. Do pay the park's small fee where you see the self-registration kiosk.

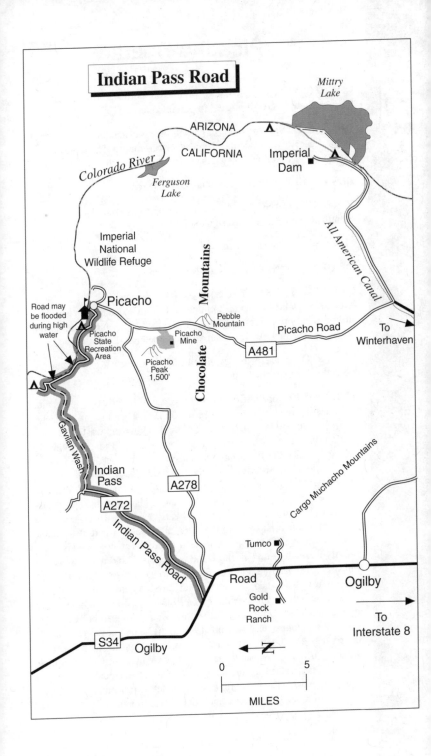

Indian Pass Road

Mittry Lake

ARIZONA

CALIFORNIA

Colorado River

Imperial Dam

Ferguson Lake

Imperial National Wildlife Refuge

All American Canal

Road may be flooded during high water

Picacho

Picacho State Recreation Area

Pebble Mountain

Picacho Mine

Picacho Road

A481

To Winterhaven

Picacho Peak 1,500'

Chocolate Mountains

Gavilan Wash

Indian Pass

A272

A278

Indian Pass Road

Cargo Muchacho Mountains

Tumco

Road

Ogilby

Gold Rock Ranch

To Interstate 8

S34   Ogilby

N

0   5

MILES

Picacho Road

LOCATION: In the Chocolate Mountains north of Yuma, Arizona. Picacho State Recreation Area. Imperial County.

HIGHLIGHTS: Here you will pass through outstanding multicolored desert scenery, reminiscent of Utah's canyon country. The route ends at the Colorado River, and includes a spur to a spectacular overlook.

DIFFICULTY: Easy, on a maintained 2WD road.

TIME & DISTANCE: 3-4 hours, or camp overnight; about 50 miles round-trip including the overlook spur.

MAP: ACSC's *Imperial County*.

INFORMATION: Picacho State Recreation Area.

GETTING THERE: From I-8 at Winterhaven: Take the Fourth Avenue exit, which connects to Imperial County Road S24. Where S24 curves sharply right (east), go straight (north) to Picacho Road (A481). Soon the pavement will end. Set your odometer at 0.

REST STOPS: There are developed campgrounds, and a shady picnic table along the overlook spur. Yuma has all services.

THE DRIVE: For the first 14 miles you will be driving on a rather uninteresting road, which is paved for 6 miles. Then the road narrows and begins to wind through an area of eroded hills and washes. Soon a vast and primeval vista of carved canyons and small ranges suddenly appears. Notice the fin, a tall and narrow slice of rock, on the left at about mile 16.4. Shortly thereafter the road passes the old Picacho Mine, a gold mine opened in the early 1890s. By mile 21.6 you will enter the 7,000-acre state recreation area. Gold is said to have been discovered along the Colorado River as early as 1862. In 1890 a large stamp mill was built close to the river, at Picacho, where its remains can still be seen. (The town was located where the campground is now.) Shortly thereafter, the Picacho Mine was opened, and a narrow-gauge railroad began hauling ore from the mine to the mill. By 1904, Picacho was home to 2,500 people. Just beyond the SRA entrance, a small road goes to the right. It's Railroad Canyon Road, a dead-end but interesting little 4-mile (round-trip) spur that follows a turn-of-the-century railroad bed to a fabulous overlook. Until 1906 trains hauled ore to mills along the river below. Back at the park entrance, go right to reach the river, where you'll find a boat launch, sheltered tables, water and toilets. Steamboats serviced a port here until 1910. It eventually became a squatters' haven. The park office is a cabin left over from squatters who once lived here. The area became a state recreation area in 1961.

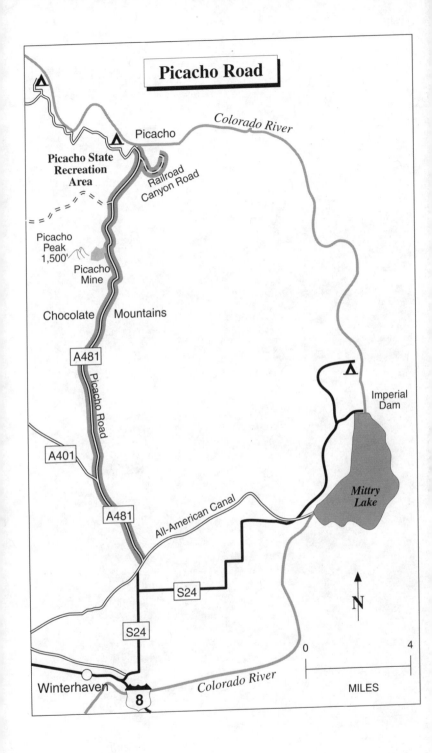

Picacho Road

Colorado River

Picacho

Picacho State Recreation Area

Railroad Canyon Road

Picacho Peak 1,500'

Picacho Mine

Chocolate Mountains

A481

Picacho Road

A401

A481

All-American Canal

Imperial Dam

Mittry Lake

S24

S24

Winterhaven

8

Colorado River

N

0   4

MILES

The Colorado River from Railroad Canyon Road *(Tour 60)*

APPENDIX

Common Desert Plants

Ocotillo

Creosote bush

Yucca

Cholla cactus

Information Sources

**4X4NOW.com &
4X4BOOKS.com**
Books, maps, advice, articles, etc.

Anza-Borrego Desert State Park
200 Palm Canyon Drive
Borrego Springs, CA 92004
(760) 767-5311
www.anzaborrego.statepark.org
*For a spring wildflower update,
send a stamped postcard, addressed
to yourself, in an envelope to:*
Wildflowers
Anza-Borrego Desert State Park
200 Palm Canyon Drive
Borrego Springs, CA 92004
For a recorded wildflower update:
(760) 767-4684

**Automobile Club of
Southern California**
(ACSC)
3333 Fairview Road
Costa Mesa, CA 92626
(714) 427-5950
www.aaa-calif.com

Bureau of Land Management
www.ca.blm.gov/caso

Barstow Field Office
2601 Barstow Road
Barstow, CA 92311
(760) 252-6000

Bishop Field Office
785 North Main Street, Suite E
Bishop, CA 93514-2471
(760) 872-4881

Calif. Desert District
6221 Box Springs Blvd.
Riverside, CA 92507
(909) 697-5200

El Centro Field Office
1661 South 4th Street
El Centro, CA 92243
(760) 337-4400

Jawbone Station
2811 Jawbone Canyon Road
P.O. Box D
Cantil, CA 93519
(760) 373-1146

Needles Field Office
101 West Spikes Road

Needles, CA 92363
(760) 326-7000

**Palm Springs—South Coast
Field Office**
690 West Garnet Ave.
North Palm Springs, CA 92258
(760) 251-4800

Ridgecrest Field Office
300 South Richmond Road
Ridgecrest, CA 93555
(760) 384-5400

**California Association of
Four-Wheel Drive Clubs**
8120 36th Avenue
Sacramento, CA 95824-2304
(916) 381-8300
www.cal4wheel.com

**California Campground
Reservation System**
(877) 444-6777

California Desert
www.californiadesert.gov
*This informative Web site is
produced by a consortium of nine
government agencies.*

California State Parks reservations
1-800-444-7275
http://maps1.ReserveAmerica.com/
static/ca4.html

Cerro Gordo
P.O. Box 221
Keeler, CA 93530
(760) 876-5030

Death Valley National Park
P.O. Box 579
Death Valley, CA 92328-0570
(760) 786-2331
www.nps.gov/deva
E-mail:
DEVA_Superintendent@nps.gov
*(Also see the commercial Web site
www.DeathValley.com for road status
and other information.)*

**Eastern Sierra InterAgency
Visitor Center**
Junction of U.S. 395 & state Hwy. 136
P.O. Box R
Lone Pine, CA 93545-2017
(760) 876-6222

Friends of the Mojave Road
Goffs Schoolhouse
37198 Lanfair Road G15
Essex, CA 92332-9799

Inyo National Forest
www.r5.fs.fed.us/inyo/index.htm

Ancient Bristlecone Pine Visitor Center
Schulman Grove
(760) 873-2500 (recording)
Open summer only.
www.r5.fs.fed.us/inyo/vvc/bcp/index.htm

White Mountain Ranger Station
798 North Main Street
Bishop, CA 93514
(760) 873-2500

Mt. Whitney Ranger Station
P.O. Box 8
Lone Pine, CA 93545
(760) 876-6200

Joshua Tree National Park
74485 National Park Drive
Twentynine Palms, CA 92277-3597
(760) 367-5500
www.nps.gov/jotr
E-mail: JOTR_Info@nps.gov

Mojave Desert Information Center
43779 15th Street West
Lancaster, CA 93534
(661) 942-0662

Mojave National Preserve
222 East Main Street, Suite 202
Barstow, CA 92311
(760) 255-8801
www.nps.gov/moja

Mojave National Preserve Desert Information Centers

Baker (at the base of the giant thermometer)
72157 Baker Blvd.
Baker, CA 92309
(760) 733-4040

Hole-In-The-Wall
Near the campground; open weekends year-round, and additional hours as posted.
(760) 928-2572

Needles
707 West Broadway

Needles, CA 92363
(760) 326-6322

National Geographic Maps/ Trails Illustrated
P.O. Box 4357
Evergreen, CO 80437-4357
(303) 670-3457 or
(800) 962-1643
www.trailsillustrated.com

National Parks Campground Reservations
1-800-365-2267
http://reservations.nps.gov

Picacho State Recreation Area
P.O. Box 848
Winterhaven, CA 92283
(760) 393-3052

Red Rock Canyon State Park
P.O. Box 26
Cantil, CA 93519
For information by telephone call the Mojave Desert Information Center in Lancaster at (661) 942-0662

Reserve America
Campground reservations
www.reserveamerica.com
California state campgrounds:
(800) 444-7275
National forest and U.S. Army Corps of Engineers campgrounds:
(877) 444-6777 or (518) 885-3639

San Bernardino National Forest Big Bear Ranger Station
P.O. Box 290
Fawnskin, CA 92333
(909) 866-3437, 3438 or 3439

Tread Lightly!
298 24th Street
Suite 325–C
Ogden, UT 84401
(801) 627-0077
1-800-966-9900

Wilderness Press
1200 5th Street
Berkeley, CA 94710
1-800-443-7227
(510) 558-1696 fax
www.wildernesspress.com

Glossary

ACSC—Automobile Club of Southern California (AAA).

Alluvial fan—A broad, fan-shaped slope of rock, gravel, sand, silt and soil deposited where a stream exits onto a plain from a canyon or gorge.

Anticline—A convex, or arched, fold in layered rock.

BLM—Bureau of Land Management, an agency of the U.S. Department of Interior. It manages millions of acres of federal public land.

Cairn—Rocks deliberately piled up to serve as a route marker.

Cherry stem—A term commonly applied to a corridor for legal mechanized travel into a designated wilderness area, where such travel is otherwise prohibited.

Desert pavement—Flat ground consisting of a layer of closely packed stones.

Desert varnish—A dark coating of iron and manganese that commonly covers desert rocks.

Fault—A fracture in the Earth's crust accompanied by a displacement of one side of the fracture with respect to the other and in a direction parallel to the fracture.

Geoglyph—A large, ancient ground design made by native people. There are two basic types, intaglios and rock alignments. Intaglios were made by moving surface rocks to reveal the lighter ground underneath. Rock alignments involved placing rocks into particular designs.

Graben—A depressed segment of the Earth's crust produced by subsidence between at least two faults.

Petroglyph—A design deliberately etched into the thin, dark varnish that commonly covers desert rock.

Playa—A usually dry lake bed.

Sedimentary rock—Rock formed of accumulated sediments.

SRA—State recreation area.

Strata—Layers of rock or earth.

Tank—A natural rock basin where water collects.

Tufa—Porous deposits of calcium carbonate usually formed around hot springs and around springs and lakes with high mineral content.

Wash—A dry streambed.

References

Automobile Club of Southern California. Various county and regional maps.

Brandt, Roger G. 1992. *Titus Canyon Road Guide: A Tour Through Time.* Death Valley Natural History Association.

Bureau of Land Management's Desert Access Guides.

Casebier, Dennis G., and Friends of the Mojave Road. 1999. *Mojave Road Guide: An Adventure Through Time.* Tales of the Mojave Road Publishing Co.

DeLong, Brad. 1996. *4-Wheel Freedom: The Art Of Off-Road Driving.* Paladin Press.

Foster, Lynne. 1987. *Adventuring in the California Desert.* Sierra Club Books.

Green, Stewart M. 1991. *Bureau of Land Management Back Country Byways.* Falcon Press Publishing Co.

Irwin, Sue. 1991. *California's Eastern Sierra: A Visitor's Guide.* Cachuma Press.

Jaeger, Edmund C. 1965. *The California Deserts.* Stanford University Press.

Johnson, Russ & Anne. 1970. *East Of The High Sierra: The Ancient Bristlecone Pine Forest.* Sierra Media, Inc.

Kirk, Ruth. 1981. *Exploring Death Valley.* Stanford University Press.

Leadabrand, Russ. 1972. *Exploring California Byways III: Desert Country.* The Ward Ritchie Press.

Lewellyn, Harry. 1993. *Backroad Trips & Tips.* Glovebox Publications.

Lindsay, Lowell and Diana. 2000. *The Anza-Borrego Desert Region.* Wilderness Press.

Nadeau, Remi. 1992. *Ghost Towns & Mining Camps Of California: A History & Guide.* Crest Publishers.

Reisner, Marc. 1987. *Cadillac Desert: The American West And Its Disappearing Water.* Penguin Books.

Schad, Jerry. 1988. *California Deserts.* Falcon Press Publishing Company.

Schad, Jerry. 2000. *Afoot & Afield In San Diego County.* Wilderness Press.

Whitley, David S. 1996. *A Guide to Rock Art Sites. Southern California And Southern Nevada.* Mountain Press Publishing Company.

Index

About the author

Tony Huegel is the author of six family-oriented guides for owners of sport-utility vehicles: *California Desert Byways, Sierra Nevada Byways, California Coastal Byways, Utah Byways, Colorado Byways* and *Idaho Byways*. He grew up in the San Francisco Bay Area, and is now an Idaho-based journalist.